MW01229360

From Fostered To Favored:

How One Man Went From Foster Care To Fortune With God At The Center Of It All!

By: Rev. Keith R. Williams

ISBN: 979-8-9906941-0-1 (Hardcopy)

First printing edition 2023

Speak Your Way To Cash®

P.O. Box 269

Flossmoor, IL 60422

www.fromfostertofavor.com

This book is an intimate dedication to the ones who have been by my side through thick and thin. To my beloved wife, Valerie, whose unwavering support and love have been the foundation of my journey. To my remarkable daughter, Ashley, and my son, Wilbert, who embody the values of resilience and faith that have carried us through. To my dear sisters, Karen, Sharon, and Steffany, who have been my pillars of strength. Your presence in my life has made all the difference.

This dedication also extends to every believer who has weathered storms and held onto their faith. I dedicate these pages to you, my fellow sojourners, for your unwavering commitment to trust in God's plan even when the path seems uncertain. Know that favor is on its way for you, just as it has been bestowed upon me. May this book inspire and uplift you, reminding you that your journey, too, can be transformed from struggle to triumph.

With heartfelt gratitude and love,
Keith

Table of Contents

Forward by Valerie Williams

In life's journey, we often find ourselves seeking answers, guidance, and blessings. We are reminded of the powerful words from Matthew 7:78, which tell us to ask, seek, and knock, for what we seek will be given, what we find will be rewarding, and what we knock upon will open doors.

In "*From Fostered to Favored*," Keith Williams takes us on an awe-inspiring journey that begins with a simple request made to God at a young age. We embark on a remarkable story that explores whether his heartfelt plea was granted or not. The revelations that unfold will captivate your heart and mind.

From an early age, Keith learned that life is a journey filled with lessons that shape and refine us. Through the pages of this book, you will witness how Keith has embraced the challenges, triumphed over obstacles, and emerged as a person transformed by the journey of life.

My own journey intertwined with Keith's on a memorable day in September 1986, when we first crossed paths. Little did I know that this encounter would lead to a love story for the ages. Over the course of almost thirty-five years, we have built a life together filled with love, cherished memories, and the unbreakable bond of best friends. Our journey is a testament to the power of love and the fulfillment of God's plan.

Life's journey is not solely about the path we tread but also the destination we aspire to reach. It is our ultimate desire to hear the words, "Well done, good and faithful servant... Enter into the joy of your Lord" (*Matthew 25:23*). In both his life and work, Keith exemplifies the essence of this scripture. Despite challenging circumstances and a unique upbringing, Keith's devotion to God and his commitment to living out His Word are remarkable.

Keith's wisdom in financial strategies, acquired through divine revelation rather than formal education, is a testament to the power of revelation knowledge. His teachings on land ownership, leaving a lasting legacy, and embracing an attitude of gratitude resonate deeply. As you delve into this book, you will discover how obstacles can often be blessings in disguise and how gratitude paves the way for supernatural blessings.

Keith shares his journey of overcoming unjust accusations and navigating through trying times. His resilience and unwavering faith shine through each chapter, reminding us all to stay focused on the ultimate destination.

This book is a guiding light for those traveling on a path that may seem uncertain. Within these pages, you will find solace in finding a safe space, understand the importance of father figures, and explore the concept of recompense.

Keith's experiences are a testament to the fact that faith grows stronger amidst adversity. As you continue your own journey, always keep your eyes on the destination. While there may be multiple ways to find God's favor, there is a narrow road leading to heaven. You will discover, through Keith's story, that God's favor rests upon you as well.

If you seek to deepen your faith and find encouragement to stay steadfast on the road less traveled, *"From Fostered to Favored"* is the perfect companion. This book will empower you to build your faith muscle, ensuring that God's favor is forever present in your life.

May your journey be blessed, and may you experience the abundant favor of God in every step you take.

Lady Valerie Williams
Wife of Pastor Keith Williams

The Thirteen Flights of Stairs

"Ask, and it will be given to you; seek, and you will find; knock, and it will be opened to you." (Matthew 7:7 New King James Version [NKJV])

I cried out to God when I was nine years old, and within twenty-four hours, God answered my prayers. I have been faithful to Him ever since.

I cried out in the stairwell, halfway up my long journey thirteen floors high, in the Robert Taylor Homes on the South Side of Chicago, Illinois. Robert Taylor was the largest public housing project built in Chicago at the time. Today, when you go to the former location of the complex, all you will find is an open field. No landmarks. No trace of the faded yellow prison-like structures that reached sixteen feet high. Just dead grass and the memories of the chaos within. Today, Robert Taylor is considered one of the most "famous failures" in American urban planning.

In the few months that I lived at Robert Taylor with my two sisters and my mother, we had to make a trek up thirteen flights of stairs every day. Robert Taylor had elevators, but they never worked. The lights barely worked. Water, electricity, a fridge of food? Never guaranteed. Each step up those thirteen flights of stairs was a test of my faith.

My baby sister hadn't even reached her first birthday when we moved to Robert Taylor; I would carry her stroller up the thirteen flights of stairs, backward. Our father was never fully engaged as a protector or provider. He was either drunk or absent, so I was in charge of caring for my sister. I couldn't move very fast up those stairs, but boy, I wished I could. What my baby sister and I saw on those stairs were things that no child should ever see. On one set of stairs, you might see a man shooting up drugs. On the next, men and women were performing salacious acts. Occasionally, I'd run into someone lying on the stairs and I wouldn't know if they were alive or dead. That was the situation at Robert Taylor. The stairs were always filthy and when you opened the door to the stairwell, the strong odor of urine permeated the space. Because the lights were often out, my baby sister and I had to navigate this journey in complete darkness. Wet, disgusting, and damp. Those was the conditions in which we lived.

I knew I couldn't shield my sisters from all they were seeing on the thirteen flights of stairs to our apartment forever. Even from a young age, I knew how dark our situation was. Hope drained every time I saw someone lying limp or foaming at the mouth. Robert Taylor got so bad that police wouldn't step foot in the complex. If you saw someone in that condition, especially as a child, you had few choices but to walk on by.

Outside of the stairwell, Robert Taylor was even more dangerous. I was a vulnerable child, just trying to protect my baby sister and my older sister, who was a year older than me. This sense of responsibility made me a target. Before I could even articulate the danger I was in, I knew I was a target. My need to protect my sisters could have quickly motivated me to walk down the wrong road. If a person with bad intentions at Robert Taylor offered to help me with safety and money and all of the basic things that I needed, I might have been more tempted to accept their offers. Would I make it to the next flight without being harmed, scared, or lured into crime? The answer wasn't always clear.

This was no place for a nine-year-old child to grow up.

Before Robert Taylor, we had lived in Englewood; and if you think Englewood has a reputation *nowadays,* just think about what it was like back then. My sisters and I moved from one unsafe environment to the next. In the earliest years of my life, I was only exposed to crime, addiction, extreme poverty, and a whole lot of activity that led children down a dangerous road.

When all you see, as a child or as an adult, is poverty, it's very hard to step outside of your situation and have faith that you can pull yourself out. All around me were people in gangs, people on drugs, and people who were completely lost. Putting so much poverty and destitution in one place was one of the reasons Robert Taylor has since been demolished. When you corral poverty and desperation in one housing complex, the people within only see hopelessness. It's no wonder that the people in these situations join themselves to other people who don't or can't show them a way out. As a nine-year-old, I still had a small flame of hope in me, but every flight of stairs threatened to snuff it out.

Fortunately, I wasn't in the Robert Taylor Homes for long.

I remember, clear as day, looking around those dim, dirty stairs, seeing my future in the people laid out on the staircase, addicted to drugs, booze, or enslaved by who knows what else. *If I keep living here,* I thought, *my sisters and I are going to be in serious danger.* Something in me, at nine years old, saw the darkness surrounding my life and rejected it. And that led me, not to take matters into my own hands, but to call up to God for help.

"Please God!" I called out. We were halfway up the stairs and had already seen drugs exchanging hands and needles going into arms. The echoes of my cries rang throughout the stairwell. "I can't make it here. I can't protect my sisters. Please, God, get us out of here!"

I carried my baby sister's stroller up the stairs to our apartment, using only the strength that my faith could provide. Twenty-four hours later, I would never have to step foot in the Robert Taylor housing again.

God listened to my call. Throughout my life, time and time again, He would provide me and my family with miracles. And so long as I live, I will never forget the first time that I talked to God, on those thirteen flights of stairs, and He listened.

"So shall they fear the name of the Lord from the west, and His glory from the rising of the sun; When the enemy comes in like a flood, the Spirit of the Lord will lift up a standard against him." (Isaiah 59:19 NKJV)

A previous pastor of mine, Bishop Henry Williamson, would always say that "faith is like a muscle." Just like we might practice a sport or a skill, we must exercise our faith so it can grow and show us the path forward. Every time I stepped into the stairwell at Robert Taylor, I had to practice my faith. I needed to have faith that I would get up each flight safely with my baby sister without being harmed. I needed to have faith that God would show us a way to safety; and because I had that faith, He did.

I wouldn't be the man I am today if I hadn't practiced faith at Robert Taylor so many years ago. Since that pivotal moment, my life has been a series of miracles, celebrations, and continued tests of faith. I've spent thirty years in the mortgage business, working as a salesman and eventually starting my own company. When I was promoted to a senior-level Vice President at Heritage Mortgage Company, I was the first African American to earn that position and my story has been featured in publications like the *Washington Post, The New York Times,* and *Crain's Chicago Business.*

Today, I am involved in multiple businesses and various properties throughout the Chicago area, but I am no longer in the mortgage business.

More importantly, I've been married to the love of my life for thirty-three years, and am the proud father of two children. My baby sister, the one I carried up the stairs all those years ago? She is now the general counsel for a large publicly-traded organization. Later in life, we even discovered that we have a third sister. We have been so blessed, but our lives have not been without moments of darkness.

The common thread through all of the trials and tribulations has been my faith. Before I was anything in my professional career, I was raised a Christian at the Carter Temple Christian Methodist Episcopal (CME) Church; the entire church embraced me as a son. Faith has carried me through my journey in the mortgage business, as an entrepreneur, as a husband, and as a man of God. In the highest and lowest moments of my life, many of which you will read about in this book, my faith has kept me moving forward.

Brought to the church by the woman who took me and my sisters into foster care, I was able to see beyond what was available in the Robert Taylor Homes. My sisters and I finally saw that there were more opportunities for making a living than getting into drugs, gangs, or prostitution. By seeing men around the church, I learned what it meant to *be* a man. The men and elders you will read about in this book were crucial to helping me develop into the man I am today.

I didn't always understand how important this exposure to men and people of faith was at the time. Heck, I didn't even understand the scriptures sometimes. Every week in those early years, the preacher shared something different and entirely new to me. I was determined, even if I didn't fully understand what the preacher was saying, to take one lesson away from the sermon to ponder throughout the rest of the week. Or, I might take away one question, and use that question to start a dialogue. As I said: faith is like a muscle. I was able to strengthen this muscle every time I sat down with the elders of the church or thought about those sermons. And these exercises of faith led me to my purpose. By operating in righteousness, and holding firm to my belief system, I was able to walk away from the darkness of my earliest upbringing and toward the success and fulfilling life that I have today.

To this day, I spend time in the Word, and I ask the Holy Spirit to lead me. As a pastor, as a father, and as a member of my community, I ask the Holy Spirit to take control of my tongue. In this book, I'm not trying to prove that I'm an eloquent speaker or the author of the next Great American Novel. The greatest compliment that someone can give me is that I took the Word, made it plain, and changed a life. That is what I hope to do for you.

I hope that this book can pay just a small bit of homage to God, to the Word, and to the people of faith who helped me along the way. I truly believe that if you see it, you can become it. I saw examples of success in my foster parent, in the men in my church, and in the community that guided me throughout my career. Maybe this book can help you see the way through to your future as well.

This book is a story about my life: I will share life-changing moments spent with people who showed me how to build a successful career for myself, how to share wealth with others, and how to be a man of faith. But at its core, this is a story about faith. Within forty-eight hours of leaving Robert Taylor, I was introduced to a woman who encouraged me in my faith. She introduced me to teachers, mentors, authority figures, and businessmen who set an example that I would follow from foster to favor. I hope that, through this book, I can be that same example to you. Whether you attend services every single Sunday or you might have lost your way, I encourage you to read this book as a way to strengthen that faith, because faith *is* like a muscle. Let us strengthen it together.

Chapter 1

My First Pancakes

"Blessed is the man who walks not in the counsel of the ungodly, nor stands in the path of sinners, nor sits in the seat of the scornful; but his delight is in the law of the Lord, and in His law he meditates day and night. He shall be like a tree planted by the rivers of water, that brings forth its fruit in its season, whose leaf also shall not wither; and whatever he does shall prosper."
(Psalm 1:1-3 NKJV)

A few hours after I called out to God in the stairwell of the Robert Taylor Homes, police officers were knocking at my door.

"Come with us," they told me, as they gathered my sisters. To be quite honest, I was terrified. No nine-year-old kid can anticipate that they are going to be removed from their home or sent to foster care. *Where was I going?* I asked myself. *Jail? On the streets? To another apartment building like this, but worse?* I wondered if I should have *specified* where I wanted to go when I called out to God. And when I arrived at my father's girlfriend's home, my sisters and I weren't exactly relieved with where we ended up.

My father's girlfriend–one of many, at different times in his life–was not excited to have us in her home. We were not welcomed with open arms. Soon after the authorities escorted us to her home, she told us where to sit and *stay*. Never mind that we were cold or dirty or needed to use the restroom; we were just told to stay where we were and stay quiet. We couldn't move around or find a bed to sleep in. Sure, my father's girlfriend had four walls and a roof. No one was shooting drugs or selling drugs or lying half-dead on the property. Our situation was slightly better than at Robert Taylor. But for the twenty-four hours I stayed at *her* house, I didn't feel like I was home. I didn't feel safe.

My father had obviously shared with a friend the problems his girlfriend had with us staying at her house. His friend told his wife, and the next thing we knew we were moving into his friend's home. Within forty-eight hours we'd gone to two different residences. What would be next? This move would land us at a three-story building on 74th and Bennett. It wasn't until I arrived at that place that I understood what it meant to "come home."

Our apartment on 74th and Bennett was in the South Shore neighborhood of Chicago. If you recognize the name of this neighborhood, it might be because you've read Michelle Obama's book *Becoming*. Michelle Robinson grew up a few blocks from me, and although we went to the same grammar school, I have more stories about her brother, who played basketball with me. South Shore wasn't the fanciest neighborhood in Chicago, but it sure wasn't Englewood or Robert Taylor. To me, South Shore was where "rich" kids lived. To me, South Shore was a breath of fresh air, an opportunity to achieve more than I had ever thought possible on those thirteen flights of stairs.

Naomi Glass was the woman who took us in at 74th and Bennett. She was a beautiful woman, with caramel-colored skin and long, black hair. Her hair was all hers, too. She smelled of Pall Mall cigarettes and had a stern look in her eye. Upon first meeting Naomi, I wasn't sure what to think. This lady didn't look warm, and I didn't understand how we ended up at her home. My sisters and I had been to our second home in forty-eight hours. Who was to say we weren't going somewhere else tomorrow?

But something was different with Naomi. She didn't issue any commands or treat us like trespassers. We weren't stuck in the corner like we were at my father's girlfriend's house. "I've got a few rules that you're going to need to follow," she said. "You're going to put God first.

You're going to honor the rules of my house, you're going to go to church, and you're going to get good grades."

"If you can do that," she continued, "we'll figure out how to make sure you have a warm meal three times a day."

She won my trust. That worked for me. For most of my life, I wasn't sure if I would have a hot meal or a meal at all. I'm sure my father's girlfriend fed us when we arrived at her home, but I will never remember any meal as clearly as the first meal Naomi fed us when we arrived at her home: she fed us pancakes. Pancakes from scratch. Fresh, warm Alaga syrupy pancakes.

I could first smell the pancakes while I was taking a bath. My sisters and I were told, one by one, to take a serious bath. By the time I had scrubbed every inch of dirt off of me, I felt like a new child. The transformation was surreal; maybe it was just the heavenly smell of a hot breakfast making its way through the house, but something told me I was finally safe. I could breathe easily. The pancakes sealed the deal for me.

When I made my way into the kitchen, I couldn't believe my eyes. That heavenly smell was coming from Ms. Glass's griddle. Along the counter were lined up the ingredients for pancakes: flour, eggs, sugar, and baking powder. I didn't even know you could make pancakes from scratch; I thought they only came out of a box. The ingredients had been mixed together in a big bowl and poured onto a large griddle in the middle of Naomi's little old stove. On a small, blue plate, there they sat: a stack of fresh, ready-to-eat pancakes.

I had never had pancakes from scratch. And I also hadn't realized how hungry I was until I felt my stomach grumbling at the sight of those pancakes.

Naomi slipped her spatula under a few pancakes in the stack and put them on a plate for me. Oh, they were so good! Fluffy, crispy pancakes that melted in my mouth. I gobbled up the first two that she gave me.

11

Then she looked over and asked, "Do you want more?" To add to my list of "firsts," I had never been asked if I wanted *more* food. I was lucky if I got enough food or *any* food! No meals had ever been guaranteed in my life. And when I did receive food, any "more" had to be shared with my sisters. We barely had enough to eat, much less an excess amount of food. "Can I have some more?" I asked. I couldn't believe my ears.

"Of course, you can!" Naomi said. "How many more would you like?" I was stunned. "How many more can I have?"

"You can have as much as you want." Naomi started to chuckle as she put more pancakes on my plate.

I can only imagine what Naomi saw at that moment: a little boy filled with hope for the first time. I'm sure my eyes widened and my toothy grin took over my face. Whatever joy beamed out of my face affected her just as much as it affected me. As she continued to put more pancakes on my plate, I remember Naomi starting to cry. I didn't know why she was crying at the time, but I was too busy shoveling pancakes in my mouth to think about why those tears were rolling down her face. She wiped her tears, picked up the phone, and called her neighbors. "Come on over to my house," she told them. "Come see these children eat." The neighbors came over and we all shared the joy of this new family forming.

From that moment on, Ms. Glass would do whatever she could to make sure that I could eat as much as I wanted, that I could have everything I wanted. She didn't mind that my father only stopped by now and again to bring us any spare cash he had on him. (He worked here and there, but by the time he finished drinking at the bar, there was no money left to spare.) Ms. Glass didn't even mind that my father wouldn't sign us over to her. She would never become our legal mother, and he could keep the tax write-offs, but she never complained. As long as she knew we were safe, had plenty to eat, and were doing well in school, she was satisfied. That's who Naomi Glass was. Eventually, we started calling her Mom.

"For by grace you have been saved through faith, and that not of yourselves; it is the gift of God, not of works, lest anyone should boast." (Ephesians 2:8-9 NKJV)

There was one other thing about those pancakes that sticks in my mind. On that counter, next to the eggs and the flour, Naomi had a dish with *real butter.* Not the margarine that comes in a tub. When she piled those pancakes onto my plate, she topped them off with a bright yellow square of *real butter.* It looked like I was eating pancakes straight out of a photoshoot!

Then, she handed me a bottle of Alaga syrup to finish the job. If you grew up anywhere but the South, you might never have had Alaga syrup on your pancakes. Putting Alaga syrup in pecan pies is a Southern tradition, and Naomi's family in Memphis always made sure she had fresh pecans and Alaga syrup in her kitchen. It's delicious in pecan pie, but my goodness does it taste heavenly on top of pancakes. Alaga syrup is sweeter than any syrup in the store. Even today, my wife keeps some Alaga syrup on hand to make pecan pies or pancakes. When I take a bite, I'm reminded of how much God has given me and how he answered my prayers when I was just a nine-year-old boy in Robert Taylor Homes.

I know that a slab of butter or a little syrup on pancakes doesn't seem like a big deal to many, but I had never had real butter. I had never tasted the sweetness of Alaga syrup. The day after I arrived in South Shore, I called up my cousin. They were living on the West Side of Chicago, experiencing a whole other level of impoverishment with stories that could fill another book. I called my cousin and said, "I think these people are rich."

"What do you mean, man?" he asked. "Why do you say that?"

"This lady gave me pancakes this morning, and guess what? She put real butter on my pancakes."

"Man, you lying!" my cousin said. "There's no way you had real butter."

"I'm telling you! It's real!" And then I told my other cousin and my other cousin. No one believed me when I said that I had had real butter. It didn't surprise me, either; I almost didn't believe my eyes when I saw that butter on my pancakes. When you grow up in the Robert Taylor Homes or on the West Side of Chicago, you're subjected to an impoverished mentality that tells you what you can and can't access. Kids like me or my cousins didn't get to eat butter. "Real food" was outside the realm of possibility. It was only for rich people. Until I saw that butter on my plate, I didn't think I would ever enjoy it in a meal, much less be able to have as much as I wanted. I was, up until that point in my life, enslaved to the idea that I might never accomplish more than my father, than my father's girlfriends, or the people who lived in Robert Taylor. Why should I be able to afford real butter? Rich people ate butter, and I wasn't going to be rich. But that's what an impoverished mentality will do to a child or even a fully-grown adult. Those pancakes, made from scratch, were my first real taste of what was possible. It changed my mentality and opened my eyes.

"And God said, 'See, I have given you every herb that yields seed which is on the face of all the earth, and every tree whose fruit yields seed; to you it shall be for food.'" (Genesis 1:29 NKJV)

Naomi Glass's cooking skills did not stop at homemade pancakes. She was always cooking something. She kept her promise: my sisters and I always had a warm meal and even some dessert afterward. Once, Naomi made a lemon meringue pie; one of those icebox pies that taste so good with a little whipped cream on top. Like the pancakes, this was my first exposure to a lemon meringue pie. Freshly grated lemons, graham crackers for the crust, PET milk...Naomi Glass did not play around with the ingredients she put in her cooking and baking! She let me have one piece. I thought the pancakes were good, but I didn't know half of what Naomi could make! I had never tasted anything so sweet and so fresh in my life.

Naomi saw the hunger in my eyes and shook her head. "Only one piece, Keith," she told me. "You can have another tomorrow."

Tomorrow? *Tomorrow?* I couldn't wait until tomorrow! That pie was so amazing that I *had* to have another piece. Something came over me– I had to have more pie! Later that night, I tiptoed out of my room and around the corner to the kitchen. That bright yellow pie with one-piece missing was waiting for me in the fridge. I snuck myself another piece, indulging in every last grain of sugar that made the pie so sweet. *Uh, oh,* I thought. Naomi told me I couldn't have another piece.

Then I thought to myself, *Well, Keith, you're already in trouble. What's the harm in having another?* One piece of that pie just wasn't enough! So, I sliced myself another piece…and another…and another. Before I knew it, the pie plate was empty. I ate the whole dang pie!

I knew what was coming to me when I woke up the next morning and saw Naomi open up the fridge. I got quite the spanking for eating that pie. That was the punishment for not following the rules in Naomi's household back then. To me, every spank was worth it. I won't take back my naughtiness that night. To this day, I don't think I'll eat anything as amazing as that icebox pie.

Naomi made sweets and desserts, but she also made delicious, filling, savory meals. Every Sunday, she would be in the kitchen preparing the meal that we would eat after the church service. While my sisters and I heard the sermon, she was back in the kitchen. The thought of those meals got me through every minute of the service back then. I knew that if I sat still and didn't squirm, I would have a big lunch waiting for me: baked chicken, all the greens, and *spaghetti.* After church, I could eat whatever I wanted, too. No one left the lunch with an empty stomach. Most people ate until they could roll themselves out!

As we ate together, the members of the community would interact. A lot of the conversations I had about faith and the scriptures took place over those spaghetti lunches. I talked to my neighbors, my Sunday school teachers, and men in the community who organized events for young men and women. These were the first people who took the time to tell me what it meant to be a man of God.

One day, my Sunday school teacher decided that he was going to take these church meals to the next level. "If you do well in Sunday school," he told us, "I'm going to take you all to a fancy lunch and you can have whatever you want to eat."

You know I did my best in Sunday school with that kind of promise! My Sunday school teacher was an honorable man, so at the end of the year when we finished our curriculum, he kept to his word and took the entire class to the Drake Hotel in Chicago. I'm talking about *the* Drake Hotel: right on the Magnificent Mile, with views of the lake and all of the fanciest neighborhoods in Chicago. But when we sat down to eat, I was confused. "Why are there two forks on my napkin?"

My teacher laughed. He was patient, showing me what each fork was for and when I needed to use them. I couldn't believe my eyes when I saw the menu: lobster and burgers and shepherd's pie and dishes I never thought I would see in real life. I might have heard about chicken livers on television, but I never expected to have them as an option. There was only one rule that we had to follow at this lunch: everyone had to order something that they had never eaten before. Chicken livers it was!

The food came, and I felt like a king. I had never sat at a table so opulent. Those people who ate caviar and wore diamonds and flexed expensive watches? Well, maybe that could be me after all. I could get used to lunches like this! When the check came, my Sunday school teacher came and sat next to me. He went through the bill and taught me how to calculate the tip, and once that was done, he handed me his credit card. I, a young boy who had a year before been living in one of the poorest housing complexes in America, was handing over a credit card to a waiter at the Drake Hotel. I'm sure if Naomi Glass saw this, she might have cried and called the neighbors over to watch it, too.

At that young age, food wasn't just food to me. Before I saw real butter on my pancakes or chicken livers on my plate, I thought food like this was out of reach. Hunger was more normal than having an unlimited amount of food to eat. My foster mother, my new neighbors, and the community at my church showed me what was possible. Because of them, I am forever blessed.

Chapter 2

A Safe Space to Learn

"Honour thy father and thy mother: that thy days may be long upon the land which the Lord thy God giveth thee." (Exodus 20:12 King James Version [KJV])

N aomi Glass grew up in a town called Prosperity, Mississippi. She was adopted by a pastor who instilled faith in her as she instilled faith in me. Her parents had one rule while living in that town: Naomi and her sisters weren't allowed to work for white people. (If anything had happened to Naomi and her sisters while working, her father knew he'd do something and end up in jail.) This rule left Naomi's family with fewer options, so they turned to entrepreneurship. They bought feathers, made pillows, and sold them on the side of the road. The girls also learned how to take in laundry, sew, and tailor clothes. All of these skills helped Naomi become a successful seamstress, making clothes for neighbors in her building and even major businesses. Long before the days of remote work, these employers allowed Naomi to work from home–she was that good at what she did.

Entrepreneurship wasn't easy, but Naomi didn't know any different. She was a workhorse. With her upbringing, being a seamstress wasn't enough. Mom also held odd jobs, babysat, and collected rent here and there to make extra money on the side. She had the means to provide for my two sisters and me with a better upbringing than what we were accustomed to, but with these blessings, she expected that we would develop the same work ethic that she had as a child.

One of the first things she did when we arrived at her home (after filling us up with pancakes and real butter) was to give us a job. Her back porch needed to be painted, so she bought five gallons of grey paint, scrapers, brushes, and rollers. "Time to paint this porch," she told us. "You pay where you lay."

We didn't mind having a job to do; in Englewood, I had held odd jobs delivering newspapers or shining shoes. If it meant I was going to get more fluffy pancakes topped with Alaga syrup, I would have painted the whole neighborhood. Naomi showed us the way, scraping, painting, and putting in the work to earn our keep. That was the type of woman Naomi was; she was kind, but she was stern. Her expectations for us came with helpful instruction, but she wasn't going to tell us twice that we needed to get our work done. Every week, my older sister and I had to contribute to the household, and when I look back on all of those odd jobs and the work I put into that house and my education, I truly feel blessed. She created a wonderfully safe space for my sisters and me to work hard and dream and grow into the people that we are today.

Mom was not the only woman who created a safe space for us in those early years. She was part of a dynamic duo with Miss Henderson, my fourth-grade teacher at Bryn Mawr Elementary. The two of them, along with many other teachers I had met throughout my years at school, taught me that I could be anything I wanted to be. Teachers have that power. Adults in the community have that power. Being encouraged by them had a similar effect as being exposed to good food and wealth: I could expand my imagination and picture myself on the path to success.

Prior to enrolling at Bryn Mawr, I had gone to school in Englewood and, very briefly, a school next to Robert Taylor. As you might have guessed, the school in Englewood was in a tough neighborhood. I remember, vividly, the dirty halls and the chaos in the classrooms. Fights would constantly break out in the school. Very little learning happened. Most of the students, myself included, were considered learning disabled and slapped with all types of acronyms that told us we were lesser.

I had friends at the school in Englewood and managed to stay out of trouble, but if I hadn't ended up in South Shore, I might have gone down an unfavorable path. My best friend in Englewood was named Alonzo, and his family was big in the streets. Every day, I came to school with no money, and every day, Alonzo's brothers would pick us up in a Cadillac and take us out to get lunch. A few other friends, who also had no money for lunch, came with us. We always went because we were so hungry.

The first few times I rolled with Alonzo's brothers, I thought nothing of it. All I could think about were the burgers I was getting for free. Sometimes, it would be the most filling meal I had all day. But I believe that I was transferred to Robert Taylor just in the nick of time. After Alonzo's brothers bought us a few burgers, they started making some questionable remarks. Expectations were starting to form in regards to what my friends and I had to do to earn our lunches in the future.

The learning environment in Englewood was bad, but the school next to Robert Taylor was profoundly worse. Every student was in the same rough situation, exposed to the same amount of crime and poverty. Fights, drugs, guns–they were all a part of the school day. Anything could happen at any minute, so the students were always on edge. By the grace of God, I was only there for a short time before I arrived at Bryn Mawr.

Moving to a new school may not be easy, but I was just relieved to live in a nicer neighborhood. I showed up for my first day of school looking fresh: Mom had bought me a beautiful, royal blue coat and matching hat for church, and she let me wear them to school. There I was, fitting in with the other students in my crisp new coat–until I got into a skirmish with a sixth grader. He knocked the hat right off of my head!

What did I do? I took off my new coat, folded it meticulously like Mom would have wanted, and set it on the ledge. She would have given me a whooping if I came home with dirt on that coat. Then, I dealt with that sixth grader the way I learned in Englewood. Word got around that

I stood up to that boy, and my time on the playground was smooth sailing for the rest of the year.

"He that spareth his rod hateth his son: but he that loveth him chasteneth him betimes." (Proverbs 13:24 KJV)

While I was able to put up a fight to prove my worthiness on the playground, I couldn't do that in the classroom. I had to study hard. Coming into Bryn Mawr Elementary, I was labeled as learning disabled. I had been written off or isolated in the past because I had that status. But that's not how Bryn Mawr operated. Every teacher encouraged their students. They made us feel as though we were scholars who were allowed to dream of success and achieve those dreams. An acronym or a label couldn't hold us back from our destiny, and we were destined for greatness.

Miss Henderson was my fourth-grade teacher, and I believe she taught me during *her* first year at Bryn Mawr. She embodied all of the values that made Bryn Mawr so special. In our first conversation, she told me not to let my learning-disabled status define me. What mattered was how hard I worked and the effort I put into my studies. I was capable of anything. "Forget about whatever happened yesterday," she said. "Everyone has a brand-new start here, in this class. You have a brand-new start." Her words had a tremendous impact on me. I believed her when she told me that I was smart and capable. Within a few months, I wasn't just catching up to the rest of the students. I was excelling.

Miss Henderson had a talent for finding what children were good at and encouraging them to pursue it. She was the first teacher I had ever met who taught that way. And, she was the first teacher I had ever met who was in constant communication with my parents. Mom and Miss Henderson were truly a dynamic duo, but their encouragement also came with the expectation that I had to work hard. If Miss Henderson gave us homework at the end of the day, Mom would be asking about it as soon as I got home. They made sure I didn't miss a single assignment.

21

Miss Henderson quickly identified that I was good at math. She told Mom and me that if I worked hard, I could be *great* at math. Mom expected me to work just as hard in school as she did painting her porch, delivering newspapers, or shining shoes; that meant studying my times tables *every day*.

For the most part, I didn't mind these exercises, but one afternoon I had had enough. Mom was acting like a drill sergeant, making me repeat my times tables over and over and over. I wasn't in the mood; I wanted to go outside instead.

"What's nine times nine?" she asked. I didn't answer.

"What's nine times nine? What's nine times nine?"

When Mom had enough of my sass, she took her twelve-inch knitting needle and popped me with it. I fell out of my chair! Not because I was hurt or because the knitting needle stung, but just because I was shocked. I got up off the floor. "Eight-one?" I said.

"That's right. What's nine times ten?"

Now, many people don't condone popping your child with a knitting needle or a good spanking, but that discipline from my Mom was just what I needed to get myself right and focus on my schoolwork. The way that I was reprimanded never made me feel unsafe or abused. My home and my school were always safe places, safer than anywhere I had been in my entire life.

When I walked to school in the morning, I felt invincible because I felt safe. Nothing traumatizing awaited me, like on the stairs of Robert Taylor. Unlike my time in Englewood, I always knew I had a warm place to stay and a warm meal to eat whenever I was hungry. My South Shore friends and I were all living in homes with happy families and we also had the support of the church. No one was trying to steer me in the wrong direction. No one could stop me from reaching any goal that I set for myself. With my mind no longer focused on protecting myself or feeding my sisters, I was able to focus on school, success, and surpassing everyone's expectations.

By the end of the year, not only was I no longer considered learning disabled, but Miss Henderson recommended that I skip the fifth grade the next year. She and my mother trusted me, loved me, and even scolded me, but all of their efforts put me on the path to becoming a more successful young man.

"Let no one despise your youth, but be an example to the believers in word, in conduct, in love, in spirit, in faith, in purity." (1 Timothy 4:12 NKJV)

Miss Henderson was just the first of many teachers at Bryn Mawr and my high school who used positivity to open doors and show me what was possible. I will always remember Mr. Carter, my elementary school basketball coach. "I'm the greatest basketball player of all time," he would tell us. Through this example, we learned how to speak highly of ourselves; and in doing so, we were able to elevate ourselves above our circumstances. Later in my life, when I was at my lowest, the lessons I learned from Mr. Carter helped me pick myself up and look forward.

Basketball was my sport through elementary and high school. I met many influential people playing basketball, and I prioritized my practice schedule even when I was looking for work. That wasn't easy for a young man to do, but I was lucky to have met Mildred Francis through my sister. Mrs. Francis was never my teacher, but she was a mentor who took an interest in me.

"I don't know what to do, Mrs. Francis," I told her one day. "I want to work, but I want to play basketball. I know I can make the team!"

"How about you take over for your sister?" she asked. My sister had worked in the book room at the high school. Mrs. Francis assured me that by working in the book room, I would be able to play basketball and bring home a paycheck that satisfied myself and Mom.

Mrs. Francis knew a thing or two about hard work. Not every student at the high school liked her; she had a reputation for being tough and urging students to work hard and go the extra mile. But she also knew a thing or two about how hard work paid off in the long run. In addition to being the chairman of the English department, she was also involved in real estate. I still remember seeing her white Cadillac Seville parked in the school parking lot; it had a big black and white wheel on the back of the car. As I helped her in the book room, she would tell me, "Keith, you're going to be a successful business person. You're going to travel the world one day." She believed in me, and she believed in my sister, too. Both of us felt confident moving forward in our careers because we had support from women like Mrs. Francis.

My sister had always wanted to be a teacher, but I had a different path in mind. When I flipped through career books and pamphlets at school, I only had one thing in mind: salary. Daniel O'Bannon, a great friend from Bryn Mawr, recently reminded me of this. He told me that, back in high school, I proudly told him, Mrs. Francis, and anyone else who would listen, "I'm going to be a mortgage banker." "Why?" they would ask.

"Mortgage bankers make a lot of money." In all of the books I read, mortgage bankers had the highest salaries. And why couldn't I be a mortgage banker? I was great at math. I could do anything I wanted to do! Mrs. Francis and Miss Henderson and Mr. Carter told me so. I had no problem believing in myself and the career that I wanted to pursue because of mentors like them.

Unfortunately, Mrs. Francis's time at my high school didn't end on a high note. One of her English students had sent out a memo riddled with grammatical errors. Even though Mrs. Francis hadn't approved of the letter, she got blamed for the mishap and drama followed. She ended up leaving the position that she had loved for so many years. I always felt terrible about it, even though I had graduated long before the situation took place.

I never thought I would see her again, but about ten years ago, I ran into her and her husband at a service station.

"Mrs. Francis!" I yelled out to her, running toward her car. "I don't know if you remember me, but my name is Keith Williams. You gave me and my sister jobs all those years ago. I just wanted to tell you what a blessing you have been in my life. My sister and I talk about all of the nice things you told us, about how we were going to be successful and travel. I have to tell you, Mrs. Francis, you were right. I work in mortgage and real estate now, and my sister is a teacher. She even won an award in Illinois recently, one of the highest honors in the state. You always told me I'd travel the world, and I've already been to five different continents. Thank you, Mrs. Francis. Thank you so much, on behalf of both me and my sister."

Mrs. Francis listened to everything I had to say, and then she turned to her husband. "See?" she said. "I told you! I told you I had a positive impact on those children!" We were all laughing, but I know that moment of gratitude was just as impactful for Mrs. Francis as it was for me.

Okay, there was *one* teacher who was not as encouraging as the rest. Her name was Miss Sheboygan. She was an English teacher. I was great in math, but I was not so great in English. I *thought I* was okay in English until I met Miss Sheboygan. She taught students in the Principal Scholarship Program, a program set up by the high school to encourage students who were performing well in school. I was in the program for math, English, and a few other subjects, too. All of the teachers in that program validated my spot in the program, but not Miss Sheboygan.

"I don't think this is your thing," she told me one day after a few weeks in her class. "Look, I don't know how you got into this program. You're going to need to go back to the regular English class. Your writing isn't at the level required for the Principal Scholarship Program."

Let me tell you: I was crushed to hear that. Now, maybe Miss Sheboygan was just having a bad day. Maybe she overlooked my writing because I, admittedly, had pretty bad penmanship. The reason why she said the things she did doesn't matter. Her words still made an impact on me, in the same way that the words that Miss Henderson and Mrs. Francis and Mr. Carter made an impact on me. I left the honors English class and I continued to slip in English. It became my worst subject!

Fortunately, this story has a happy ending. Years later, I ran into Miss Sheboygan at a Chicago Bulls basketball game. By this time, I was doing well in my career and was able to put in some money for floor seats. I was in my first Armani suit for the occasion. There she was, Miss Sheboygan, in the stands. I still remembered some of the things she said to me in that class that tore me down, but I knew I had the last laugh. I reintroduced myself to Miss Sheboygan, and I let her know that, despite the doubts she might have had, I was doing very well for myself. I don't hold a grudge against this teacher, but I certainly felt like it was a big deal being able to show her how I had made it in life.

Everything that I have accomplished in my career has been due to the work ethic and the ability to dream that my education provided me. The teachers, the coaches, and my mother all had a hand in telling me that, despite where I had come from or how I was first brought into this world, I could make a name for myself. Success, happiness, and a beautiful life were all accessible to me. The life I live today was just a mere dream so many years ago, but because I had permission to dream, I'm able to tell you about my story today. That's the beauty and the miracle that I experienced at my school and my foster home. That's the power of having a community of supportive adults around a child. I couldn't be more thankful for those who supported me.

Chapter 3

Father Figures

"Let your light so shine before men, that they may see your good works and glorify your Father in heaven." (Matthew 5:16 NKJV)

I rarely saw my biological father once I arrived in South Shore. He stopped by, here and there, but although he refused to give us up for adoption, he remained absent. The example that he gave me was not one I wanted to follow, especially after moving to South Shore and meeting the men that worked and lived in the community.

Mom understood the importance of introducing me to these men. We had to make up for lost time; my sisters and I had spent too many years only being exposed to poverty, crime, and men who didn't show up for their children. Through Mom, we were exposed to new people: professionals, law enforcement officers, entrepreneurs. And these men graciously guided me, without any judgment of where I came from. They belonged to the middle class, displaying a type of excellence that I had not seen before. I could be excellent, too, they reassured me. Through these introductions, my mother continued to drill into us that we did not have to follow the path that led so many people to places like Robert Taylor Homes.

The men she introduced us to became father figures to me. They taught me how to be a man: how to prosper, how to treat women, how to love God fully, and how to be a father to my own children. Without them, I don't know if I would have been able to get married, *stay* married for over thirty years, and raise the successful children that I have today.

A lot of these men were mentors through the Boys to Men program. The church set this program up because they knew that young boys needed to see and talk to men who were checking all the boxes and succeeding in their lives. Although these meetings took place through the church, we didn't censor ourselves. I learned lessons about sex, girls, and dating that I had never broached with my biological father and would be too embarrassed to talk about with my pastor.

My interactions in the Boys to Men program were not limited to the church itself. The men in the program made themselves available to me so that I could come to them when and if I needed anything.

One such man was Mr. Lightfoot. Now, I don't know if he is at all related to Lori Lightfoot, the mayor of Chicago, but at the time he was a mentor and a fascinating man. Mr. Lightfoot was a detective, a great example of a man enforcing the law in his own community. He and his family would spend time with me, celebrate my birthdays, and support me as I made my way through college.

Mr. Lightfoot also stepped in when I was having a tough time. In college, I had a "Fix It Again, Tony" type of car, if you know what I mean. It was always in the shop. One day, I drove down the expressway and the axle popped right off. I saw it shooting out in front of me on the road! I took the car to get a new axle and an engine tune-up. I hadn't had a ton of experience with car repairs, so when the mechanic told me that he needed $1,000 upfront, I handed him the money and left the shop.

Week after week, the mechanic brushed me off. He didn't fix the car when he said he would–he didn't fix the car at all! After a while, I reached out to Mr. Lightfoot for advice. I had spent all this money and I wasn't getting my car back. What was I going to do?

"Be ready at 10:00 a.m. tomorrow," Mr. Lightfoot told me. "I'm going to pick you up and we're going to handle this." No questions asked–Mr. Lightfoot was ready to help. The next day, we went down to the shop and Mr. Lightfoot handled the situation. I was able to get some of my money back, and although my Fiat never *fully* functioned to my liking, I was able to get back on the road, drive to work, and continue taking care of my sisters without being short $1,000.

Another man in the church, Mr. Bias, was a McDonald's owner. His daughter was in my Sunday school class and he was a regular at the Boys to Men meetings. No one at the meetings dressed terribly, but I remember how Mr. Bias was always *impeccably dressed.* Crisp suits, nice watches, everything! And his car was always shiny and clean. When you stood next to him, you realized you probably needed to get a better wardrobe.

Mr. Bias made a decent living for himself, but he also spent time shopping for clothes and finding the best prices on the highest-quality materials. He and a few of the other men were kind enough to show me where to buy clothes, how to shop, and how to show up looking like the money you wanted to make. These lessons are often taken for granted by children and young adults who have steady fathers in their life, but they meant the world to me. Everything, from tying a tie properly to interacting with the police and respecting authority, was all a part of the Boys to Men program.

We learned how to negotiate and we learned how to dress, but most importantly, we learned about the scriptures in the Boys to Men program. We learned how to be men of faith. There was no better example of how to be a man of faith than Oliver Hightower.

Mr. Hightower was a modest man, no taller than 5'7", with bright skin. He was the assistant principal at one of the schools in our district, the head of the Sunday School program, and he also was an inventor. Above all, he was a disciplinarian. He was tough, but he was steadfast in his faith and wanted to instill the same values in the boys that he mentored. Every time that I met with Mr. Hightower, he would check in with me about passages of the scripture.

Reading it wasn't enough; we had to memorize it. There was only one time that I failed to memorize the passage he had suggested to me. As I fumbled through the verses, I could see the disappointment in his face. It cut me like a knife to know I had let him down. He was an amazing man who just wanted the best for us; the least we could do was memorize a passage. I never let myself slip again.

I looked up to Mr. Hightower; I truly loved this man. He was an embodiment of what it meant to be a man of faith. He didn't have a car, yet he would walk five miles every Sunday just to get to church. Well into his 90s, he would walk five miles each week, and even though he was robbed once on his walk and members of the church started driving him, he was willing to put that amount of effort into his faith.

If you ever hear me reciting scripture in any of my sermons, you can thank Oliver Hightower and the men at Boys to Men that pushed me to work hard, practice my faith, and become the man of God that I am today.

"But someone will say, 'You have faith, and I have works.' Show me your faith without your works, and I will show you my faith by my works. You believe that there is one God. You do well. Even the demons believe— and tremble! But do you want to know, O foolish man, that faith without works is dead? Was not Abraham our father justified by works when he offered Isaac his son on the altar? Do you see that faith was working together with his works, and by works faith was made perfect? And the Scripture was fulfilled which says, 'Abraham believed God, and it was accounted to him for righteousness.' And he was called the friend of God. You see then that a man is justified by works, and not by faith only."
(James 2:18-26 NKJV)

There were a lot of men in the church and the community who made me the man I am today. But I would be foolish not to dedicate significant time sharing the impact of Wilbert Thomas. One of the former police officers in our community described him best: "Wilbert Thomas is an angel in our midst." There's no better way to say it! Wilbert Thomas was a presence: over 6'6" with a bald head and a booming voice. When you heard him talk for the first time, you would swear that a volcano was rumbling somewhere in the distance. Wilbert probably had the deepest voice of anyone I ever met.

That voice led me through many important conversations in my life: about faith, about basketball, and about being a man. I remember clear as day asking him about a woman I had been dating. We were on track to get married, but I was feeling apprehensive. While some men might have gone to their fathers or brothers to ask for advice, I went to Wilbert. And I listened to Wilbert, too.

"Look," I told him. "I don't think I want to marry this young lady, but I'm trying to do the right thing. Help me out here."

"Boy," he said. His voice rumbled and I already knew what he was going to say. "Don't be no fool. You don't marry nobody you don't want to marry. Who's making you get married? Only you get to decide."

I was such a young boy then. Wilbert's advice empowered me to make the right decision and break off the relationship. (I made the right choice, and met my wife soon after this relationship ended.) When Wilbert talked, young people listened. And thank God they did, because Wilbert had a gift for guiding people in the right direction.

Young people in the community truly loved Wilbert. He didn't just give great advice on serious matters. He was joyful, he was personable, and he loved to have fun. Every summer, he'd buy a bunch of balloons and get out the hoses for big water balloon fights. We were dumping buckets on folks, splashing around, and pulling pranks. The first time I brought my wife over to his house (a woman who Wilbert, this time, encouraged me to marry), I had to warn her about what was coming. "I hope you don't mind getting your hair wet," I joked. If there was one thing I knew about women, it was not to mess with their hair. Wilbert knew this too, but he didn't care. Anyone who stepped foot in his backyard for the first time was going to be pranked, and that usually meant a bucket of water dumped over their head.

Wilbert's backyard was always filled with friends and young people who needed a safe space in the neighborhood. He was a magnet for youth in the community. Not only did he have room on his property to run around, but he also had a basketball court. Wilbert was from Arkansas, and one of his brothers played Division 1 basketball. Athletic ability was a part of his family's DNA. Wilbert was a phenomenal basketball player, a real-deal athlete. And when I looked to the stands during every one of my high school basketball games, Wilbert was there. He never missed a game, for me or for many of the young men that came around to his house.

Our church put together a basketball team, and he was the coach. We'd play all day and then get ice cream in the evenings. The basketball games at his house were no joke. Nobody liked to lose. We put everything that we had on the court, even though we were just playing for bragging rights. It wasn't uncommon for someone to finish the game with a bloody nose or scrapes. We weren't being violent—we were just playing with everything that we had. And with his sharp elbows and immense strength, whoever was on Wilbert's team usually walked away with those bragging rights. The guy was an ox but moved like a gazelle.

I met Wilbert when I was a freshman in high school, although I saw him frequently at church. No matter what time you arrived at church on Sunday, you could always count on Wilbert to be at the front of the church with his hands raised high. He didn't care who was around or what people might think; he put his whole soul into praising the Lord. The first time you saw Wilbert, you might think he was being obnoxious. He wouldn't care if you told him that. He would start praising louder! He had nothing on his mind but gratitude for what the Lord had provided for him, and that gratitude was contagious. After a minute or two of watching him, you would put your hands up and start praising, too.

Wilbert was a man who lived his faith in everything he said and did. He was blessed, and he was a blessing to so many. He and I had many conversations about faith.

He broke down the Word so beautifully, and he broke it down in a way that proved that intellect wasn't even enough to grasp the deepest meaning of the scripture. Wilbert had a high school education; I don't know if he ever considered college. But every time I would come home from college, he'd find a way to stump me. I thought I was smart, but no one could beat Wilbert when it came to having a conversation about the scripture. "Revelation trumps information seven days a week," he would tell me. How could I argue with that? We'd go back and forth, back and forth, but Wilbert always got me in the end.

"Man is justified by works, and not by faith only." That was Wilbert. He taught me that your feet need to be a part of your faith, that you always need to be walking in the right direction with your whole body and soul. He didn't just talk the talk. He walked the walk, helping everyone in the community with whatever he had and whatever he could do for them.

He helped us immensely when Mom got sick during my first semester of college. I had always balanced my education with work and taking care of my sisters, but Mom had always been around to provide for the family. As she transitioned from care giver to needing care, I realized that I had to get my butt in gear and seriously work to make money and be the head of the household. I was no longer just working to have some extra money in my pocket. I needed to pay the rent–the full rent.

After Mom passed, I went to him for advice on looking for an apartment. My sisters and I couldn't afford much with the income we brought in. When we looked at the market, we realized that we would be going in the wrong direction, closer to where we came from than how we were living in South Shore. Wilbert wouldn't let that happen. He insisted that we come live with him.

Wilbert made a decent living. He dug holes for gas companies and connected pipes. The job didn't sound glamorous, but you would never know it by the way Wilbert dressed. He was one of the many men that helped me pick out clothes, tell a quality suit from a cheap one, and save money along the way. His income was modest, but he was smart about the way he spent it; that's how he was able to provide for his family and the community.

Wilbert's house wasn't grand. He had maybe 1,200 square feet to his name that he shared with his wife and daughter. Wilbert didn't mind a crowded house. He built two small rooms in the basement to accommodate me and my baby sister. We all had some privacy in the house and we were able to live comfortably and safely until we got back on our feet and could move into our own apartments. And he didn't stop there, either. I eventually bought my own house in the suburbs to raise my family. Until the day that he left to be with the Lord, Wilbert was there to cut the grass. I tried to pay him, but he wasn't looking for payment or anything in return. He just liked to drive out to the suburbs and take care of my grass.

How can you repay a man who has given you so much? I asked myself this question all the time. One day, I couldn't sit back and just let my "thank you" be enough. Wilbert told me that he was driving out to see his mom in Arkansas and would be gone for a few weeks, and I knew this was my chance to help out a man who had helped me throughout my whole life.

"Well, when are you coming back?" I asked him. "If you can wait until the weekend, I'll be happy to make the drive down there with you."

Wilbert shrugged me off. "I don't know when I'll be back, son. But don't you worry 'bout a thing. You stay here and keep this grass looking nice." He had just retired from his job, so he had the freedom to come and go from Chicago as he pleased.

"Before you go," I told him, "I want to give you something." At the time, I had been doing very well in my career. I was well past the point where I was working to have some extra money in my pockets; my pockets would have been too full. So, I pulled out $2,000 and tried to put it in his hand.

"No, Keith," Wilbert said in his booming voice. "I can't accept this."

"Please, Wilbert. It's nothing to me. Take it and enjoy yourself."

"No, no, no."

I had to smile. "Hey, man, you're messing me up." I had a plan. He was going to accept the money.

"What do you mean?" he asked me.

"If the Lord tells me to sow a seed into somebody's life, and that person doesn't let me, it's not impacting you–it's impacting me. You are blocking my blessing, Wilbert."

Got him.

"Well, if that's the case," he said, "I'll take it."

"Good. I didn't want to have to force you!"

That $2,000 was the only time I would ever get to bless Wilbert; it was a fraction of how he blessed me. As he drove down to Arkansas to visit his mother, he fell asleep behind the wheel and crashed his car.

Wilbert's funeral was unlike any funeral I had been to in my life. All of 79th street was blocked off because so many gas trucks from the company escorted their employees to the church. Every person he

36

worked with showed up. The president of the company was there. Thank God there were no gas leaks or problems during his funeral because all of Chicago would have had no one to fix the issue!

Every person, whether they worked with Wilbert, played basketball in his yard, or saw him at church, had beautiful stories to tell about him. He had an impact on so many people. We laughed at all the pranks he pulled and reminisced about the way he showed compassion to others. If he saw a man on the street, he would bring him in for a hot shower, new clothes, and a good meal. If a family was having hard times, he would be the first person there to deliver meals or whatever the family needed. He provided for his own family and was always there to bless somebody else.

My son was also in attendance at Wilbert's funeral. Those who know me know my son's name: Wilbert. Yes, I named my son after Wilbert Thomas, the father figure I never thought I would have when I was growing up.

Where would I have ended up if I hadn't met men like Wilbert Thomas, Oliver Hightower, Mr. Bias, or Mr. Lightfoot? What kind of man would I be if I hadn't attended a program like Boys to Men? I don't like to ponder these questions for too long, because I instinctively go back to those thirteen flights of stairs at Robert Taylor Homes. When people like my biological parents couldn't step up and show me the way to prosperous adulthood, members of my community took my hands and guided me in the right direction.

Like most children, I didn't know what type of person I was going to be when I grew up. Unlike most children, I was exposed to environments and situations that showed what type of person I did *not* want to be when I grew up. All I saw and all I knew was negativity. I dreamed of something else, but at first, I didn't know what those dreams actually meant. Positive influences, at my foster home, at school, and at church, filled in the blanks for me. They showed me how to dream. They also showed me how to live that dream, and how to become a prosperous man who lives by the Lord, and who provides for his family. There isn't a better dream to be living!

Chapter 4

My First Lessons in Financial Literacy

"The rich rules over the poor, and the borrower is servant to the lender." (Proverbs 22:7 NKJV)

When I first started attending Carter Temple CME Church, I felt like an outsider looking in. I felt like a kid looking into a bakery, with his nose pressed against the window, desperately wanting all of the sweetness inside. Standing on the outside looking into the lives of the men I saw at church, I saw riches. I saw men who were rich, monetarily, in spirit, and in love. These men attended church every week with their families, praising the Lord and setting a fine example for their children. That's the type of man that I wanted to be.

Although I was a long way away from starting a family of my own, I had the opportunity from an early age to provide for my family through hard work. The first jobs I had in my life started as a way to buy bread and keep some money in my sisters' pockets, but what I didn't know was how those jobs would shape who I am today. My first jobs taught me important lessons about what I wanted to do, what I didn't want to do, and the importance of strategic relationships.

I was working long before I could get a permit. At seven years old, I started delivering newspapers for a local African-American-owned grocery store near my house. My family was still in Englewood back then, and money was not plentiful. I needed this job so I wouldn't have to use food stamps.

My biological mother couldn't give me cash to buy food. All she had was food stamps; and even at seven years old, I hated using food stamps.

Now, there's nothing wrong with using food stamps, but they didn't feel right in my hands. I would walk into the corner store for bread and milk, and I could see how the people working in the store looked at people like me using food stamps. They looked down on anyone who was getting financial assistance. I remember, one day, I tried to buy some food with food stamps and I just couldn't do it. I used the little bit of money I had in my pocket so I could save myself the embarrassment I felt using them. When I got home, I handed back all the food stamps that my biological mother had given me.

"I didn't use the food stamps," I told her. "Why didn't you use the food stamps?" she asked.

"It made me feel poor."

My mother was furious. "Everybody around here is poor!" I got a whooping for not using the food stamps, but I didn't regret making that decision. Something inside me told me I was not a person who was going to use food stamps.

Fortunately, a man who owned another grocery store in the area caught onto the fact that I barely had enough money for food. He would never have judged me for using food stamps, but he understood my struggle. For each mile that I delivered newspapers, I got $1. The payment never covered all the expenses of caring for my sisters. When the man who owned the grocery store saw that what he paid me was all my family had to buy groceries, he got an idea. To this day, I believe that little idea changed my life.

He started charging me interest.

Baby formula was expensive at the time, and it was just one of the many things my family needed. Loaves of bread, bologna, formula, and lemon cookies added up to around $10 each week. I only delivered enough newspapers to have five or six dollars to spend.

"Here's what I'll do," the owner told me one day when I was searching my pockets for change. "You give me that six dollars for your groceries, and you will owe me four dollars. I'm charging one percent interest on all that you borrow." I was able to walk away with the food I needed to feed my family, counting how much money the grocer had "lent" me and what I needed to pay the next week. If there were no papers to deliver, I would be given odd jobs around the store to help pay off the balance I owed. I took whatever job he offered so that I could settle my debts.

Did the owner of the store really keep a ledger of all that this seven year-old child owed him? Did we ever settle up when I moved to Robert Taylor? I don't believe so. I know now that this man was extending kindness to me and teaching me all about what it meant to be a borrower who is in service to the lender. In the same way that I knew I didn't want to use food stamps, I learned important lessons from my time delivering papers. I learned that I didn't want to spend too much time being on the borrowing side of things. When I grew up, I told myself, I was going to become a lender.

Years and years later, I would reflect on the money I had "borrowed" at the grocery store. It was after I had taken out some hard money loans with friends of mine. All the risk, once again, was on my side. I was a servant to the lender. The pressure was on me to pay back the lenders quickly and get out of the deal as soon as possible. I couldn't help but laugh, thinking about how I was feeling that same type of pressure that I had experienced while I was a seven-year-old boy working at the grocery store, looking for ways to work odd jobs, and pay back what I owed. Because I learned how lending and interest worked way back then, I was less likely to make mistakes borrowing money later in life.

My time working at the grocery store ended when my family was relocated to Robert Taylor. I wanted to keep working, even if that meant borrowing money from employers and paying interest. But I couldn't.

41

Going to work meant that I would have to walk up and down those thirteen flights of stairs and put myself in danger more frequently. At eight years old, I knew my experiences were different than many people who lived in Robert Taylor, but I remember so much of my experience as fear. Fear of seeing all of the people who were doing drugs, performing lewd acts, or getting into criminal activity in the stairwell. Fear of violence. Fear of people who wanted me to go down the wrong path in life. That fear paralyzed me, preventing me from going out and working to provide for myself and my sisters. I'm glad I only had to endure that fear for a few short months.

When I arrived in South Shore, my foster mom always had us doing odd jobs around the house, like painting the deck. I also had a more formal work arrangement with her husband. Since my biological dad was in and out of my life, my sisters and I called Naomi's husband "Uncle Earl." Uncle Earl was distant, not always around, and not like the men who showed up at the church each week with their families. He was not a man of faith. But Uncle was able to teach me valuable lessons and give me work before he died.

Uncle owned a body and fender shop, and he was successful. He was the reason that Naomi was able to own her house and even support herself after he died. The garage was filled with old cars that Uncle had bought and fixed up. Any time Naomi needed a little money after Uncle passed away, she would sell one of the cars and be able to pay the bills. I saw the importance of having those assets tucked away even though they were not as valuable as a home or a retirement account.

I spent some time working at the body and fender shop. I earned about $15 or $20 a day and learned about cars. One of my first jobs was sanding the cars. Oh, did that job hurt my hands! I would be standing over the cars, wearing just a mask that didn't do a great job at keeping out paint fumes. After a while, I would take a break and see that my hands were bleeding.

"Uncle, my hands are bleeding from sanding the cars." "That means you're doing it right," he said. "Keep moving."

That's the kind of man Uncle was. He told me to keep working, and I did. He wasn't abusive, but he wasn't warm. My hands would heal after a hard day's work. He knew that. What was more important was the lessons I learned while working in the shop. The more I worked at the body and fender shop, the more I learned about cars.

The more I learned about cars, the more I learned that I *didn't* want to work with cars. That motivation pushed me to work harder for the rest of my life. The only way that I was going to avoid working with my hands in the shop was to excel when I was working in the office.

"Watch and pray, lest you enter into temptation. The spirit indeed is willing, but the flesh is weak." (Matthew 26:41 NKJV)

Uncle was murdered two years after I arrived at his home. After he died, I wasn't able to work for the body and fender shop. Instead, I got a job shining shoes. Everyone came into the shoe shop to get their shoes shined: church-going people, businessmen, and pimps. The shop was in a rough neighborhood, so it wasn't unusual for a dope dealer to sit down, get a shine, and leave me a big, fat tip.

Working at the shoe shop taught me a lot about people and their spending habits. Not everyone tipped me well, and those that did tip well didn't always have the best motives. I remember getting $20 and $50 tips. I knew these guys worked on the wrong side of the street. They made me think of Alonzo's family sweetening me up with free lunches. To my eleven-year-old self, those $50 tips felt like winning the lottery. Even a $20 tip made my whole day. But the men who were throwing this money at me were more likely to be pimps and drug dealers than your average church-goer, and I knew that they were trying to plant seeds in my mind. If they could convince me that they were successful, maybe I would abandon my post at the shoe shop and do whatever they told me to do. I never did let those seeds in my mind grow into anything dangerous, even though the dope dealers and pimps tried their hardest to convince me that they could make me rich. But the richest men in my life weren't the men giving me $20 or $50 tips. The richest men were the men at church.

By the time I started working in the shoe shop, I had been in foster care for two years. The changes I had experienced were nothing short of a miracle. Teachers were no longer telling me that I was always going to be behind–now, they told me I was going to excel. Food was always on the table and I didn't need to take out a loan to buy lemon cookies for myself and my sisters. I had come so far in life and I didn't want to do anything that took me back to where I came from.

My life in foster care allowed me to not only look back on my life in poverty, but also to look forward. I knew that I wanted to make good money, eat in nice restaurants, and have a nice car. What's more, I was finally seeing men who had accomplished these things without compromising their morals. They owned Mercedes and drove their whole families to church. They proudly shared, with me or the pastor or with anyone who would listen, what they did for work. Living a rich life as a person of faith was possible. I didn't need to rely on pimps and dope dealers to make the money that I envisioned for myself.

If I had been more vulnerable, that shoe shop might have been the first step down a bad path. But it wasn't. I kept on the straight and narrow, looking for honest work.

At thirteen, I was ready to move on from the shoe shop, so I started working at clothing stores. One was a clothing store that was willing to pay me under the table. The store was three miles from my house, but the distance didn't matter. I was happy to walk there before my shifts and sometimes get a ride back from Mom at the end of the day. When another clothing store called Zayre was hiring, I put in an application. I didn't know anything about work permits, so I just lied about my age.

They accepted my application, and I was able to start paying Social Security. I continued working for Zayre on and off for many years, taking time off to play basketball or work in the school book store with Mildred Francis. Work never took precedence over high school or basketball, but it was always a priority.

"Do not despise these small beginnings, for the Lord rejoices to see the work begin, to see the plumb line in Zerubbabel's hand." (Zechariah 4:10 New Living Translation [NLT])

Basketball became more of a priority when I started attending college. Sports taught me about work ethic in the same way that my time at Zayre or the auto body shop taught me about work ethic. I had never been the tallest or the biggest guy on the team, but I learned that if I played hard, I would always have a prominent position on the team. I was willing to play hard, practice often, and not back down from anybody. Thanks to all the work I put in, I had actually been recruited and offered scholarships at a few schools. They weren't Division 1 schools, although I'm sure I could have kept up with those players back in the day!

Wilberforce University in Ohio was the obvious choice after touring some of my other options in the Midwest. It was the first college to be owned and run by African Americans associated with the African Methodist Episcopal (AME) Church. Meanwhile, the other schools that wanted me were white as snow. There wasn't an ounce of diversity in those schools, so I felt more comfortable in a place like Wilberforce. If I had been desperate to get out of my situation, maybe I would have leaned more toward Wisconsin or one of the bigger schools that had their eye on me. But I wasn't desperate. I wanted to be comfortable and close enough to my family that I could drive back and forth when I was needed.

College athletes might appear to have a glamorous life, but let me tell you something: their schedules are grueling. I don't know how a lot of athletes these days get a fine education *and* prepare for playing professionally. It's hard to do both; it's possible, and I know many people who have done it, but it's hard. I never bet my education on going pro, so I spent less time in the gym and more time working. Keeping money in my baby sister's pocket was more important to me than catching the eye of professional recruiters.

I found myself looking for work that accommodated my schedule, just like in high school. There weren't many flexible jobs, so I ended up starting my own business. Wilberforce was in a small town, and college kids had a hard time going anywhere because the buses in the area stopped running at 6:00 p.m. Luckily, I didn't have to take the bus because I had a three-speed AMC Hornet to get me around town.

People always told me I was so lucky to have a car. After I heard this from enough people, I realized there was a need and a market where I could bring in some good money. My car wasn't glamorous: there were places where it was totally rusted out and had holes in the bottom portion. But the car was dependable and ran on little gas. Any time someone on campus needed a ride past 6:00 p.m., I was there to drive them. All they needed to do was throw me $5 and a slice of pizza. Around the holidays, I would cram people into the car for the five-hour drive back to Chicago for a higher price. And when I wasn't around to drive people, I asked my roommate to do the driving and gave him a cut of the earnings.

Before there was Uber, there was my raggedy AMC Hornet.

I continued to operate this ancient version of a ridesharing business until Mom got sick. At first, I thought I could go back and forth to Chicago from Ohio, but her condition progressed quickly. When she passed, I moved back to Chicago permanently, dropped out of Wilberforce, and began attending Chicago State University. Basketball was no longer a priority; I had to be the head of the household and support my sisters in a larger way. But I had experience as an entrepreneur, and I was not afraid to work hard.

"Commit your works to the Lord, and your thoughts will be established." (Proverbs 16:3 NKJV)

No employers wanted to give me more than thirty-five hours of work a week because they would have to pay me benefits. So, I worked multiple jobs throughout college, with no benefits but enough money coming in to pay the bills.

One of these jobs was at United Parcel Service (more commonly known as UPS). Originally, I had been hired as a loader and an unloader. It was backbreaking work. I understood why so many guys came in, worked for thirty minutes, and walked out the door. I thought back to the days of working in the body shop with Uncle. Nope. That wasn't going to be me. That wasn't my future. I wasn't going to be able to do physical labor for thirty-five hours a week and still get to my other jobs. So, I hatched a little plan.

After I was hired, I walked over to the man who looked like he was in charge. "Sir," I asked him, "Do you have any computer jobs around here?" "Do you know anything about computers?" he asked. "Well, yes I do!"

I didn't know anything about computers, but this man took me into his office where a few computers were stationed on desks. Fortunately, he didn't know that much about computers, either.

"As it turns out," I told him, "these are a bit different than the computers I'm accustomed to using. Can you just show me what needs to get done?" He showed me what the previous employee had been doing on the computer, and I was able to learn it quickly. That's how I got a job in the dispatch office, which supported me throughout my time at Chicago State.

I was always working two or three jobs at a time, but another constant was my position at First National Bank of Chicago. I got this job right out of high school, and I was always rehired when I was back in the area. Whether I worked on weekends or during the summers, I always showed up on time in my nice necktie, ready for work. Working at the bank was going to be my first step toward getting that job as a mortgage banker, the job I had wanted since I learned how much money I would get paid.

I got the job thanks to my high school principal Mrs. Lightfoot, the wife of the Mr. Lightfoot who helped me out when I was having car troubles. Before I went off to college, I told her that I wanted to be a mortgage banker. She picked up the phone right then and there.

"Is this Clark Burrus?" she asked.

Clark Burrus was well-known around my neighborhood in Chicago. His name was always in the newspaper. He was the chairman of the Chicago Transit Authority and worked for a bank called First National Bank of Chicago. Talk about rich men in our community–I couldn't believe how much this guy made, and I couldn't believe Mrs. Lightfoot was calling him! I later learned that the two knew each other through a bridge club.

"Clark Burrus, I'm going to need a favor from you," Mrs. Lightfoot said. "My godchild needs a job for the summer. He's just *wonderful.* But he needs a job where he can learn some things and start building his skills."

I could hear Clark Burrus asking Mrs. Lightfoot about what I was doing for work. "Well," she said, "he's still in high school. But he's going off to college this summer. A job with you would be a great way for him to learn more about banking and get started on his career."

Mr. Burrus wasn't impressed, but Mrs. Lightfoot was persistent. "No," she told him, "you're going to find something for him to do." She hung up the phone, and a few weeks later I was working in the offices of First National Bank of Chicago.

When I worked at First National Bank, I found myself on the outside looking in again. The bank was downtown, a short walk away from the Drake Hotel where I tried chicken livers and first paid the tab on an expensive meal. When I got off the train, I quickly found out that the Drake Hotel was not the only place in Chicago for fine dining. There were so many amazing restaurants downtown! I wanted to try everything, even if that meant eating chicken feet, sheep's tongue, or other strange dishes. All I wanted was the experience of sitting down at one of those nice tables and ordering a good meal for myself.

Instead of being on the outside looking in at church-going people, I was looking at a much more elevated version of wealth: bottles of wine that looked like they were $100, waiters in pristine coats, tiny displays of sweets, and cakes that looked divine. Working at First National Bank of Chicago was going to be my first step to affording these meals and sitting in these restaurants. And it all happened because of people like Mrs. Lightfoot. She had a friendly relationship with someone who could offer me a great opportunity at the bank.

I soon realized that relationships made a big difference. It was one of the many lessons I learned from my earliest jobs. Strategic relationships with people at church, at school, or at work always gave me access to bigger and better things. Strategic relationships would keep me out of the jobs that I didn't want to work and in the jobs that paid enough for me to support my family. After I graduated college and started taking further steps toward my dream career, I learned that strategic relationships were just a piece of the puzzle. Faith, seizing opportunities, and even miracles helped me step into my dream career.

Chapter 5

Miracles in the Mortgage Business

"That if you confess with your mouth the Lord Jesus and believe in your heart that God has raised Him from the dead, you will be saved." (Romans 10:9 NKJV)

Throughout college, my salary was never enough to reach the level that I had dreamed for myself and my family. I was like a hamster running in a wheel and all I could do was run faster and faster. When money became tight, I just took on another job. I drove mail trucks, continued working at UPS, and took whatever work Clark Burrus could give me on weekends or over the summer. Sleep wasn't a priority. If I got four or five hours of sleep a night, I was lucky.

One afternoon after work, I was dead tired, but I was just awake enough to believe that there had to be a better way toward the career I wanted for myself. "I'll figure it out tomorrow," I told myself. "For now, I need to go home and get some sleep."

I believe that the angels were ready to drive my vehicle that day. Before I was halfway home, I could feel myself falling asleep. This wasn't uncommon at the time, but I would tell myself that I just needed a coffee or a nap to keep me alert. I exited the expressway with the intention to pull over and sleep. Instead, I woke up driving through a green light. I had fallen asleep behind the wheel.

I was scared to life. People say that they are scared to death all the time, but with the help of the angels, I wasn't heading in *that* direction. When I woke up and realized that I had been sleeping, I decided things needed to change. I needed to find a job that would keep me healthy, awake, and satisfied. My life was going to improve; it had to. Otherwise, I was going to fall asleep again and really hurt myself.

As I pulled over, I realized I had no idea where I was. My brain fog, or maybe it was the angels, had led me to a random street on the West Side of Chicago. Once parked safely on the side of the road, I took a nap. "There has got to be a better way," I told myself when I woke up. I directed my plea to God. "Please," I said. "Show me the way out. Just like you took me away from those thirteen flights of stairs, please take me out of this grueling schedule."

God told me to get out of the car, so I did. A newspaper stand was on the sidewalk next to where I had parked my car. Right on the front page of the newspaper, there was an ad for a job. "$100,000 Potential Yearly Income," the ad said. Well, alright. I talked to God, and God answered once again. I was going to apply for this job and make $100,000 a year. A few days later, I was suiting up for an interview.

"Eat thou not the bread of him that hath an evil eye, neither desire thou his dainty meats: For as he thinketh in his heart, so is he: Eat and drink, saith he to thee; but his heart is not with thee." (Proverbs 23:6-8 KJV)

The room where the interview was held was big. There had to be around 100 people all applying for this job! But I wasn't worried. God had brought me here for a reason. I sat down and started filling out the application on the clipboard provided.

One of the lines on the application said, "Income requirement." I came to the job interview because I wanted $100,000, so I wrote down "$100,000 minimum." I circled it twice and handed in my paperwork. All I had to do was wait for my name to be called.

Ten minutes later, a man came out of one of the offices to address the room. He was a well-dressed African-American male with impeccable hair and nice jewelry. I was impressed. I wanted to make enough money to look like this guy. "Who is Keith R. Williams?" he said. I raised my hand and he told me to follow him into his office.

The office was just as pristine as this man's outfit. I could see all of Chicago from a big window. Yes, this was a job I wanted.

"Do you wonder why I called you in here," he asked, "before calling any of those other people?"

"Well, yes, that does seem a little strange," I told him.

"Take a look at this. Can you explain this to me?" He pulled out my job application and pointed to the income requirement. "Why did you circle this? And why did you put a minimum of $100,000?"

I looked him square in the eye. It was time for me to be bold. "Look, man, if this job doesn't pay that type of money, don't waste my time. I need sleep. I'm working two full-time jobs, a part-time job, and I'm going to school full time. I really don't have any time to waste here. I'm looking for a better way to live."

The man put his hand up. He heard the nerves in my voice. "Man, calm down," he said. "Take your time. Listen, everybody else in that room put a maximum of $30,000. You blew everyone out of the water with your income requirement, which is why I called you in here. I was intrigued. Let me help you out, man." He put on his coat and told me to follow him out the door.

Across the street from the office was a bookstore called B. Dalton's. "I'm going to show you some things about the mortgage business," the man told me. "But first, you have to get your mind right and your spirit strong." He led me over to a section filled with self-help and motivational books. *Think and Grow Rich* by Napoleon Hill. *As A Man Thinketh* by James Allen.

This man told me that by looking through these books, I would be able to follow through on what I envisioned for myself. I thanked him, chose a few of the books, and let him buy them for me. As I started going through those books later that evening, I got a call that I was hired.

I didn't work in that position for long; the management was engaged in some practices that made me uncomfortable. But I will never forget that interview because it opened a very special door for me. One of the books that I picked that day was *The Richest Man in Babylon* by George S. Clason. The name caught my attention. I knew Babylon from many, many stories in the scripture. The city of Babylon was a symbol of power and splendor, but the most studied stories about Babylon were cautionary tales about the destruction of sin. And here was this self-help book referencing the same city as it gave cautionary advice to people looking to build their wealth.

The more that I looked through these books, the more I recognized lessons and advice that mirrored scripture. *As a Man Thinketh* was another example. I found the bible verse and the book's message to be another cautionary lesson that I applied many times throughout my career. These self-help books didn't always quote scripture directly, but I couldn't deny the similarities. I was hooked.

As I continued reading and cross-referencing scripture, I found myself reflecting on other life lessons that had led me to my present circumstances. I thought about Mom's work ethic, about the temptation I faced in Robert Taylor, and about the people who tried to take advantage of me when I was vulnerable. I thought about all of the men in my life who guided me and even those who showed me what not to do. The combination of these life experiences, along with these self-help books and the scripture, helped me grow my faith tremendously. Everything good led to God.

"And let us not grow weary while doing good, for in due season we shall reap if we do not lose heart." (Galatians 6:9 NKJV)

I was determined to make it in the mortgage business. My first job, although brief, opened my eyes to what was possible. I found a new job in the industry, agreeing to a paycheck based solely on commission. Wilbert had told me that I could stay in his home for as long as I wanted, but I assured him I was going to be able to pay the bills while living in the new apartment I had started renting. The apartment was nice and had a view of the lake, and I could afford the rent. This new salary was a huge leap for me: I had gone from working three jobs at once to working only one job. I felt like a king.

To bring in commission, I went around to different offices "leasing" a computer program to real estate brokers. Brokers used the program to check the status of the loans that we offered them. The software was saving them tons of time they would have otherwise spent on the phone, and we were getting more loans because of the convenience provided by the program.

I was working around the clock for this company, bringing in commission and learning the ins and outs of the mortgage business. This was a significant new chapter in my life, and I was succeeding, too. The program sold itself, I just needed to take the time to build strategic relationships with brokers and help them set up the computer while we closed the deals on the loans. Everything was going well.

I thought my life was perfect until I started building relationships with other loan originators. Don't get me wrong. I got along well with other loan originators and operators. But when I told them what I was doing for work, they were blown away.

"How much work do you do?" they would ask me.

"Oh, I don't know, thirty transactions a month?"

"Man, you must be making a fortune!" they would tell me. At the time, $50,000 a year felt like a huge step up from the hourly rates I had made before, but I wouldn't have called it a fortune. I was making my rent payment, but I had little to spare because most of my paycheck was going to support my baby sister.

"What do you mean?" I would ask. "I'm not making a fortune. How much do you make?" These guys had nice cars and nice clothes. As it turned out, they were making four times as much as me! "Man," they would tell me, "you should be making $300,000 a year with all the business you're bringing in!"

After having this conversation with loan originator after loan originator, my luxurious paycheck became an embarrassment. Most people were making a base salary along with a commission per transaction. Me? I was working solely on commission, and making a fraction of their earnings. I didn't want to tell people about my compensation structure anymore. I wasn't proud of what I was bringing in. Learning that I was on the raw end of the deal certainly discouraged me, but I'm thankful I made relationships with the men in my industry who were transparent about what they were making and what typical rates were for people who were closing as many deals as I was. Who knows how long I would have gone on, making $50,000 a year when I could have been making far more?

My relationship with the owner of the company's daughter also encouraged her to advocate for me. Our relationship was strictly a friendship, and she saw how her dad was holding back from paying me what he should.

"Dad," she had told him, "you're going to lose this guy if you don't change the way he's paid. He deserves to be making much more money than this." But her dad never wanted to reconcile the books. Instead of paying up, he tried to pay me back in small fragments. "Here's $1,000," he would tell me after his daughter pressured him a few times. "What about $1,500?"

I was stuck. When I took the time to sit down and calculate what this man really owed me, it was significant. He was dragging his feet. I deserved more, but I also needed to pay my rent. But if I walked away, I would have to go back and work for UPS or a job that took me two steps back. For a short period of time, I took the small repayments. In my spare time, I looked for a place that would treat me fairly. Once I had a new job, I was going to leave.

Finding a new job was a struggle, but not because I was young or inexperienced. When I told people the amount of business I was doing, they didn't believe me! I had been working day and night to make my small salary, using this computer program that saved time and brought in tons of business. But I didn't give up, and thank God I didn't.

Eventually, a group of guys saw the potential in me. They saw how accessible I was and how much drive I had for closing a deal. I also had a cell phone, which was uncommon. Remember, this was back in the day! No one had cell phones. I was spending a fortune each month on my phone bill, but I viewed it as an investment in my career. The investment paid off; I was easier to reach than any other loan originator in the city. Real estate brokers move fast. If you can't close the deal within a month, the deal is going to go to someone else. Deals were usually held up by slow communication. Most people would get a page about a deal but couldn't get back to someone immediately because they couldn't get to a phone. I could call brokers right back and have the deal closed by the end of the day.

Technology was always pushing my business forward, whether it was those wacky computer contraptions or cellular phones. That is how I got into the mortgage business: strategic relationships, fast communication, and investing in the technology that allowed me to be accessible to others. I was paying a higher phone bill than I do today, but every penny was worth it because my numbers were astronomical.

"My brethren, count it all joy when you fall into various trials, knowing that the testing of your faith produces patience. But let patience have its perfect work, that you may be perfect and complete, lacking nothing. If any of you lacks wisdom, let him ask of God, who gives to all liberally and without reproach, and it will be given to him. But let him ask in faith, with no doubting, for he who doubts is like a wave of the sea driven and tossed by the wind." (James 1:2-6 NKJV)

My dream position was with Heritage Bank Corporation. They were bringing in big money. The loan officers there had the Mercedes that I had been dreaming about for years. I wasn't going to have to struggle to make rent–I could buy my apartment if I was able to get a job there! But I didn't get the job immediately. I was running into the same objections: no one believed how much business I was doing. They didn't realize that the majority of my business was coming from the white neighborhoods throughout Chicago, which is where the big companies preferred to do business in those days. I didn't let these objections deter me. I *was* going to work for this company, drive a Mercedes, and make good money for my family. I had the skills and I had the relationships to make it happen.

I had grown especially strong relationships with two white guys who had been working with me. They saw how accessible I was and how hard I worked. We were a dream team!

"Look," I told them. "The guys at Heritage Bank Corporation are making a fortune. We sell way more than they do! We should go in and talk to them together." They agreed with me. Walking into Heritage Bank Corporation with these two men behind me allowed me to walk through the door.

I showed them the numbers we were doing, and with two white guys backing me up, I was taken more seriously. All three of us were cut in on a deal, although I was still considered someone who would just "tagalong" behind the white guys. This hurt my pride, but I was used to it at that point. When I got home that night, I made a promise to myself:

I was going to destroy every salesperson there in terms of business. I was going to blow everyone out of the water.

And I did.

The position at Heritage Bank Corporation was a culmination of a lot of things: hard work, humility, building relationships, and investing time in myself to learn about the mortgage business and what it took to make me successful. Above all, I had dreamed about this career since I was in high school.

Around the same time that I decided I wanted to be in the mortgage business, I was in a program called the Urban League. It was my version of summer camp because my foster mom couldn't afford to send me away to summer camp. One of the men in the Urban League told a story about dreaming. He came upon a house that he didn't own, knocked on the door, and told the owners that one day, he was going to own that house. And he did! Dreaming, he taught me, was a way that you could strengthen your faith, just like a muscle. If you can visualize something, you can ultimately have it.

I dreamed about my career in the mortgage business. I dreamed that I would have enough money to support myself and my family. And I dreamed about owning a Mercedes.

As I was proving myself at Heritage Bank Corporation, I would spend my Friday lunch breaks at the Mercedes dealership. I would sit in the cars, dreaming about owning one. The first few times I visited the dealership, a salesperson would approach me; after a while, everyone knew to leave me alone.

I kept dreaming and dreaming, working and working, until I got married. And then, as a wedding present, my boss called me into his office.

"I want to congratulate you on getting married. And because your numbers have been so impressive, I want to get you a gift. Let me know what you want."

This was my chance. "I want a car," I told him.

It wasn't unusual for people at the company to get cars as bonuses, but no one ever got a Mercedes. One lady got a BMW, and a few people got Cadillacs. I didn't want a Cadillac; I had already been battling enough stereotypes working in the mortgage business. Getting pulled over on the way to a deal does not set you up for success. Fortunately, my boss knew cars. When I told him that I didn't want a Cadillac, he understood. He knew that no one at the company had received a Mercedes, but he also knew I had done great work.

He reached into his pocket and he pulled out a card. "Take this to the dealership and get the car of your dreams."

I *ran* to the dealership. All of the salespeople were so used to ignoring me that I had to flag someone down! I saw an African-American salesperson walking by, and I pulled him aside. "I need this car, in this color, and I need you to send it down the street to the AMG place for some nice rims." All those years of dreaming gave me enough time to know *exactly* what I wanted. I already knew how the car felt, smelled, and all of the bells and whistles that came inside it. Did I test drive it? Nope! But I was ready to buy.

"Let's bring you to the finance guy," the salesperson told me. "Nope! Give this card to the finance guy. Tell him to call my boss–he'll take care of everything."

When I put that key into the ignition and heard my Mercedes run, my dream had finally come true. Dare I say, it was a miracle. Those early days in the mortgage business truly came full circle when I drove that car. I wouldn't have taken the risk and found my first job in the industry if I hadn't almost run my car off the road out of exhaustion. God had a hand in leading me to fulfill the dreams I had been dreaming since I was a child. And although my trials and tribulations were far from over, this time in my life confirmed that faith and dreaming could lead me to anything that I wanted.

Chapter 6

The Love of My Life

"He who finds a wife finds a good thing, and obtains favor from the Lord."
(Proverbs 18:22 NKJV)

You didn't think I was going to tell you about my wedding present and not tell you about my wedding, did you? The story of how I ended up married to the love of my life deserves a chapter of its own. After all, it is the greatest love story ever told. You can't tell me otherwise!

When I met my wife, life was good. I was coming up in the mortgage business, and I was certainly confident: I was finally making money, I dressed nicely, and I had nice things. Before I had the Mercedes, I had a Volvo, and I was proud of that Volvo. It wasn't new, but it was the best car I had owned to that point. The Volvo even had a car phone. I know I sound like a dinosaur saying this now, but at the time, I was living large!

One night, I wanted to show off the Volvo, so I drove over to Chic Rick's. Chic Rick's was one of the first African-American-owned nightclubs in downtown Chicago. And although I spent plenty of time studying scripture and reading books like *As a Man Thinketh,* I also wanted to go out and have a good time. Plus, I knew I looked good. That night, I had on a nice sweater, some Run-DMC leather Adidas pants, and a nice chain. I looked *prosperous.* And I knew other people looked at me and thought that I was prosperous, too!

I pulled up to the club, handed the valet my keys, and told him to keep the car parked in the front. Everybody at the club needed to see my ride–I was just that confident.

Inside, the club was hopping. Everyone who came to Chic Rick's was on the dance floor that night: old classmates, neighbors, guys who I played basketball with. My future wife was also there, but I didn't know it until I got on the dance floor.

People don't always believe in love at first sight, and I'm here to tell you that it's possible. I looked across the room at Chic Rick's and I fell in love. Valerie was wearing a purple suede dress, her hair was meticulously laid, and she had just enough jewelry to highlight her natural beauty. She was the most gorgeous woman I had ever seen in my life.

There was only one problem: she was dancing with somebody else.

Valerie had decided to go to Chic Rick's that night for her 23rd birthday. She was *supposed* to go with an ex-boyfriend. "I want to go dancing," she told him.

"I'm not going dancing," he said. She tried to ask again and he refused. But before he hung up the phone, he told her, "I hope you meet somebody tonight."

She sure did! Years later, her friends and I still laugh about this. I have to thank her ex-boyfriend for saying what he said. I don't know if he understood the power of what he was speaking. Words clearly have power!

I didn't know anything about Valerie's ex-boyfriend or what he told her until *many* years later. At Chic Rick's that night, all I knew was that I was standing in the same room as the most beautiful woman on Earth. The guy that she was dancing with couldn't hold a candle to me–at least, that's what I thought at the time. I was a brash, young thing. And I had a Volvo with a car phone!

I wasn't going to go another minute without trying to catch this beautiful woman's attention, so I made my way across the room and stood close enough to where she could see me. I'll admit, I made my presence known. I stood, and I waited. The "other" guy was confused, and I could see him getting nervous. "Is that your boyfriend?" he asked Valerie.

"No!" she said. "I don't even know him."

She was about to know me. I waited until the song was over, and then I gently touched her hand and asked if she wanted to dance. She accepted.

"What brings you out on this beautiful evening?" I asked her.

"It's my birthday."

Without missing a beat, I told her, "And I'm the gift."

She laughed, but I wasn't finished yet!

"Look," I told her, "you're so extremely beautiful and quite impressive. But I'm more popular than Michael Jordan, and you made a good choice dancing with me!" She kept on laughing at my arrogant self, and she didn't dance with anyone else the rest of the night.

I even tried to invite her over to my house, but she wasn't having any of that! She gave me her number and left the club with her girlfriends. She probably didn't think that *she* had just met her future husband, but *I* knew that I had just met someone very, very special.

"Again I say to you that if two of you agree on earth concerning anything that they ask, it will be done for them by My Father in heaven. For where two or three are gathered together in My name, I am there in the midst of them." (Matthew 18:19-20 NKJV)

When I met Valerie, I knew I wanted to be in a relationship. I had gotten to a point in my career where I could comfortably support a wife and children. The men at my church had been so inspiring in the way that they loved their wives and respected the spiritual covenant of marriage. I wanted to follow their lead and obtain *all* the riches that I had dreamed of.

Together, as Valerie and I started to date and build our relationship, we modeled our communication and partnership after the role models in our lives. I was still living with Wilbert Thomas when I met my wife. Wilbert and his family led their lives with integrity, kindness, and joy. No one in Wilbert's family left home or arrived home without a hug or a kiss. He and his wife embodied the idea that you were not supposed to go to bed angry. After living with them for a short period of time, I knew that *that* was what I wanted in my life. With Wilbert's family serving as an example, I was able to approach all of the ups and downs of being in a relationship in a more positive way. To this day, I don't go to bed angry and I don't leave the house without embracing my wife; and we certainly don't leave without praying together.

I remember the moment that I decided I was going to marry Valerie. We had been hanging out for some time, doing what young people do. Friday had come around and I was ready to go dancing. So, I called up this beautiful woman I had been dating and I asked, "Valerie, you want to go out tonight?"

"Why don't I just cook you dinner?" she asked.

I was stunned. I thought she was just playing around! This woman was too pretty to *also* know how to cook. No woman that I had dated or hung out with in the past really knew how to cook. But after teasing her a bit, she convinced me that she was serious.

"Just come over and I'll make you something. What do you like to eat?"

By now, you already know how much of a blessing this question was to me. I had grown up poor, so I ate anything and everything. The only thing I didn't like eating was bananas–but that story is for another book. I told her, "Make me whatever you like."

I walked through the door of her house and thought I was walking into heaven. The aroma of candied yams, crowder peas, and macaroni and cheese hit me before I could take two steps. The steak was still cooking in the oven but the green beans and cornbread were ready. Valerie handed me a glass of fresh lemonade and led me into the kitchen. For a moment, I forgot I was living in Chicago: the table was laid out perfectly with all the dishes and all the fixins' of a good, Southern meal. I thought for a moment that Valerie had some older lady working behind the scenes to put this dinner together! But no, it was all her.

That dinner rivals every single dinner that I have ever eaten in my life. Everything I tasted was better than the dish before it. I remember starting to sweat. I was a confident young man, but I didn't want Valerie to know that I was legitimately in love.

And then she pulled out the peach cobbler.

The dessert of the evening was a *homemade* peach cobbler. Picture the prettiest peach cobbler you've ever seen. Valerie's was better. The woven crust on the top was thick, and oozing butter. (There goes that butter again!) The bottom felt like dumplings. There was no way that I could hide my love for this woman. She was going to be my wife.

But I didn't have that magic, surprise proposal that you read about in romance novels. Valerie proposed to me *first*. She might have a different perspective on how this happened, but until she writes a book about our relationship, you're just going to hear the story from me.

After two years of dating, Valerie and I took a trip to Atlanta. The trip was full of laughs and love and good food. On our final night of the trip, we had dinner at a restaurant with a 360-degree view of the city. We were on top of the world, and we felt like it, too. In between courses, Valerie just dropped the question.

"Do you want to get married? You know, I might want to get married." She said it so casually! I had to make sure I was hearing her right.

"I don't know what you're asking me. Are you asking me to marry *you?* Or are you asking me if I want to get married in general?"

She rolled her eyes. "Oh, you know what I'm talking about. Let's go look at some rings."

I know my memory of the night might be a little fuzzy, but I swear, at that moment, the whole room moved. My world was coming together and changing at the same time. Our conversation wasn't romantic like in the movies, but it perfectly encapsulated the beauty of our relationship. Valerie had always been forthright and confident, keeping me on my toes. In return, I had always strived to take care of her. I wasn't going to properly propose without a ring. So, after that conversation, we picked out rings and made our engagement official.

A few years after we got married, we celebrated the birth of our daughter, Ashley, and the birth of our son, Wilbert. And a whole 30+ years after we shared our vows and made a sacred commitment in front of the Lord, we're still going strong. Valerie still keeps me on my toes, and I still do everything in my power to take care of her and my family. She still makes me those elaborate dinners of crowder peas and greens, even if it does mean that dinner begins at eight or nine o'clock. That's just the type of amazing woman that she is.

"Behold, how good and how pleasant it is for brethren to dwell together in unity! It is like the precious oil upon the head, running down on the beard, the beard of Aaron, running down on the edge of his garments. It is like the dew of Hermon, descending upon the mountains of Zion; for there the Lord commanded the blessing–life forevermore." (Psalm 133:1-3 NKJV)

Our marriage was made easier by the examples that we followed in our lives. We grew together, both as partners in a marriage, as parents, and as people of faith. But that doesn't mean we didn't face tough times.

My wedding gift was a Mercedes, and I even bought one for my wife shortly after we got married. We had money in the bank, hitting the goals that I had set for myself when I was a young child reading about the mortgage business in the library. At the time of my marriage, I had reached the top of the mountain; but as you'll learn, I took some tumbles later in life that brought me to where I am today.

At every step of my journey–climbing, falling, and getting back up again–Valerie was there. And because the scripture had set an example for how she should and should *not* conduct herself, she was able to serve as a guiding light when I was in the darkness.

In the scripture, Job's wife undergoes a transition, not unlike the one my wife and I faced. Within minutes, Job and his wife lost their lifestyle. Their children, possessions, health–poof, it was all gone. Job even breaks out in boils. Job's wife doesn't take this the right way. She looks at him and asks him to curse God and die.

What happens when Job pursues his faith and everything is restored to him? In the scripture, Job's wife isn't there to enjoy it. Her children come back to life, and yet she is not there to witness the miracle. The story of Job's wife is a cautionary tale, both about faith and marriage. We learn that a wife should speak of the man she wants her husband to be until he becomes it. It's an idea that is not unfamiliar in self-help books like *Think and Grow Rich*. I'm sure there is even a self-help book for singles that gives this same advice.

The virtuous wife, according to the scriptures, knows this. She knows this and doesn't harp on her shortcomings but looks forward to the future that she wants to have. Words have power, remember? This doesn't just apply when you're looking for a relationship, like the night my wife's ex's words had power and she met me. Words also have power when you are trying to maintain a relationship. And the power that you put behind your words, positive or negative, leads you in that direction.

Valerie knows this and practices it every day. I remember one moment in particular when I was at my lowest. My net worth was plummeting because the market had turned the world of real estate on its head. The world had been taken out from underneath me. Everything I had earned was quickly being drained, leaving me high and dry. That day, I didn't even know how I was going to pay the electric bill. On a grander scale, I didn't know where to turn or how to earn back everything I had lost.

In my despair, I turned to the Lord. And this took strength because my faith was being tried at that moment. I was praying in the corner of my house that I reserve for prayer and studying the scripture. On my knees, I tried to reach God with the same desperation that I had felt all those years before.

God had a plan for me, I was sure of it. I was fortified in my faith, despite the trials I knew I was facing. I reminded myself that I was going to emerge victorious and prosperous. But I kept on praying. Valerie knew how to reassure me at this time. We didn't need to have a long conversation about our finances or our faith for her to know exactly what to do. She came over to a where I was praying and put her hands on my shoulders.

"Your seed will sustain us," she said.

"Valerie," I asked, "what do you mean?"

"The seeds that you sowed yesterday will bring us a harvest in our time of need."

Her message was simple, just as the parable of the seed is simple. In both the biblical and the natural sense, the seed is a symbol of growth, hope, and prosperity. *Where* you sow your seed determines what you are able to reap. Jesus explains this parable in Luke 8:11-15 (NKJV):

"Now the parable is this: The seed is the word of God. Those by the wayside are the ones who hear; then the devil comes and takes away the word out of their hearts, lest they should believe and be saved. But the ones on the rock are those who, when they hear, receive the word with joy; and these have no root, who believe for a while and in time of temptation fall away. Now the ones that fell among thorns are those who, when they have heard, go out and are choked with cares, riches, and pleasures of life, and bring no fruit to maturity. But the ones that fell on the good ground are those who, having heard the word with a noble and good heart, keep it and bear fruit with patience."

My wife didn't have to say all this. She knew it, and she knew I just needed a gentle reminder. All she needed to do was place her hand on me and reassure me of everything we had sown together. Throughout our relationship and throughout our lives, we were intentional about where we sowed seeds. Although our crops were not bearing fruit in the monetary ways that we had anticipated, we heard the Word. We had noble and good hearts. All we needed now was patience.

Eventually, that patience paid off, but I wouldn't know that for many years. At the time, what I needed was just her hands on my shoulders to help me feel better. With Valerie's support and faith, I could look up. And if I could look up, I could get up and go forward with my life. Her words were what it took to start making progress once again. And no matter what has happened or what will happen in my life, Valerie will be there to guide me in the right direction. Our relationship embodies Psalm 121: 1-2 (NKJV), *"I will lift up my eyes to the hills–from whence comes my help? My help comes from the Lord, who made heaven and earth."*

All those years ago, on the dance floor at Chic Rick's, I told Valerie I was her gift. And I do believe that my words were powerful and that my value was something that would be of interest to her. I was a young thing, and although my intentions weren't entirely holy in Chic Rick's, I know that the Lord led me to Valerie to write the greatest love story ever written. I am her gift, and she is mine. Thirty years later, we have grown into the people of faith and the parents that we are today, still loving and communicating with each other with the same passion and power that we had when we first met. We still embrace each other. We still impress each other. We are still kind to each other. That's the key–kindness. We have sown seeds of kindness into everything that we do, and in return, we have been immensely blessed.

As I continue to tell my story, you will read about some of the hardest times I have ever faced. Keep the faith; there are no sad endings here. With the faith of the Lord and the love of my wife and family, the trials and tribulations that I have faced serve as stepping stones and proof that those who sow seeds of faith in the good ground will bear fruit. If life ended tomorrow, I wouldn't have anything to complain about. Because I have sowed the seeds of faith, and those seeds have sustained our family.

Chapter 7

Money Doesn't Come with Instructions

"Cast your bread upon the waters, for you will find it after many days."
(Ecclesiastes 11:1 NKJV)

Now, let's go back to that Mercedes. The reason I ended up getting a Mercedes as a wedding present is because I had built a strategic relationship with the boss who would end up signing the check. The relationships I built during that time in my life not only taught me how to grow wealth, but also taught me how to hold onto it.

Money doesn't come with instructions, and it takes a community of people to even tell you that instructions exist. I was fortunate to build that community in my early career.

I wasn't surprised when my boss bought me a Mercedes. Don McNeil was not the most approachable man: he was a blue-blooded, wealthy, White Anglo-Saxon Protestant (WASP). He was very conservative and everybody knew it. But the thing about Don is that, throughout my time at Heritage Bank Corporation, we found a way to bond: cars. I knew I could talk to him because I was making him a ton of money, and as we bonded over our love of cars, we became friends. He invited me to his house to see his whole collection of cars.

Don was one of the many people who helped me see that wealth wasn't just about individual transactions. With the right mindset and the right strategies, wealth was something that you could *grow*. He didn't share any references to the Bible or talk about sowing seeds when he took me under his wing and taught me about wealth, but he offered me guidance. I began to ask him about money and how I could accumulate wealth. His advice helped me immensely.

Don taught me about the stock market and how to look for the best purchases. When I told him about Wilbert Thomas and his job position at the gas company, we discussed how the stocks in his company were moving. I was inspired by him to work with Wilbert and the guys at the company. Often, these guys needed money quickly. I needed a way to grow my portfolio and build wealth. So, transactions were conducted. I would discount the stocks by 10 percent because they weren't moving, and I would provide men who held the gas stocks with the cash they needed. As I was setting up the sale, I would consult Don. He knew how to ensure that the transactions couldn't be reversed and he had guys at the bank ready with all the signed paperwork. Once the sale was conducted, Don advised me to put them in a safe deposit box and hold onto them for later.

I thought I was living large when I was first working at Heritage Bank Corporation, making six figures and riding around in a Volvo with a car phone. Men like Don showed me that this was just the beginning of my journey. He guided me through everything I needed to know about loans or collateralization, interest, and APRs. He opened my eyes to everything I could do in real estate, both as a banker and as someone who owned properties. You don't know what you don't know, and as I worked closely with Don, I realized just how much I didn't know about investing and growing my portfolio. If I was going to be able to grow wealth the way that the *really* wealthy people around me grew wealth, I would have to talk to those people and learn from them directly.

"He who keeps instruction is in the way of life, but he who refuses correction goes astray." (Proverbs 10:17 NKJV)

Soon after I got a Mercedes as a wedding gift, I bought a Mercedes for my wife. By the time I had kids, I had a *third* Mercedes. Each one had a custom vanity plate: "LNDING1," "LNDING2," and "LNDING3." I would drive a different one to church each Sunday.

One of the newer men to the church, Andy Davis, caught sight of my three Mercedes. Andy had a Bentley, and he was impressed by what he was seeing. He asked Wilbert Thomas (because everyone in the church knew Wilbert), "Who has those three Mercedes? I have to find out what this man does for a living."

Andy Davis and I became business partners, but not before he offered some wisdom.

"Man, I have to tell you something. You don't need three Mercedes. You don't even need two! That's a bit excessive."

Andy was a lot like Don McNeil; he knew how to buy a car. He taught me how to buy a car that wasn't going to bleed him dry. I quickly learned that I was buying new cars that immediately depreciated in value. Don and Andy were smarter than that–they bought old cars that appreciated in value and put the rest of their money in an index fund. They still had something shiny in the driveway, it just wasn't shiny and new.

I didn't know all of these tricks until I met men like Andy and Don. Early in my career, I thought I was doing the right thing by buying something shiny and new. "Fake it 'til you make it" was my motto, and I was living it. I was doing all the right things to grow my wealth, but the seeds were still seedlings and I wasn't ready to harvest. I was pretending like I had a bountiful harvest. Andy helped me see that you could look wealthy without giving away all of the money you had just earned. Putting five figures on a credit card each month wasn't the way to grow your wealth.

Another person in my life who taught me this lesson was a man named Leon. Leon and I started working together because he was a money lender who financed real estate for investors and developers throughout the city of Chicago. He and I would often discuss the viability of several neighborhoods throughout the city; Chicago property values could change quickly block by block. Our business relationship turned into a real friendship.

The mortgage business blessed me with the chance to have numerous interactions with people like Leon and Andy and Don, from various communities and classes, and of various races. Friendships and relationships like these offer the wisdom of different perspectives and access to opportunities that I otherwise might not have had.

One of these important interactions happened with Allan Edelson. Our first conversation led to Allan inviting himself over to my house to talk business. I was a little nervous to let someone I had just met into my home to talk real estate, but I knew that our partnership had the potential to be profitable. I told him where I lived and he came over.

Allan pulled his Honda Accord next to my Mercedes. He got out, wearing raggedy shoes and a tattered pair of blue jeans. This guy didn't *look* like someone who had a lot of money. At the time, I thought all people with wealth drove Mercedes and Bentleys and lived in extravagant houses. Allan lived in a modest condo in the historic Gold Coast district in Chicago. I knew that condo wasn't cheap, but he wasn't making a huge display of the money he had in the bank.

The more I got to know Allan, the more I realized that he could afford any car he wanted and any home he wanted. He just chose something more modest, as his parents and grandparents had done. He only wrote big checks when he knew he was going to get something back from that big check: loans, investments, etc.

Allan was one of the first people to send me over to the bank to pick up a significant check; he helped me through my real estate journey. But the real lessons he taught me were about what people did with their wealth. His family had multiple generations of wealth, and by the time that wealth reached him, he knew that living an opulent lifestyle just sent that wealth down the drain. I hadn't learned that lesson yet, because money doesn't come with instructions.

As I learned from people like Leon, Allan, Andy, and Don, I tried to bestow my wisdom onto my family. My true education in wealth didn't come from my undergraduate degree–it came from the people who knew how to walk the walk and talk the talk. With every person that I met, I confirmed the importance of relationships. Where would I be today without Andy Davis or Don McNeil? I don't know, and I don't want to know; Life-long relationships make our journey in life a lot less rocky.

So, when it came time for my baby sister to go to school, I stressed the importance of strategic relationships.

"You have to go to the best university you can go to," I told her, "but it's not about the education. You can get a fine education anywhere, but you have to consider where you are building relationships. The most helpful people are going to be at the best schools you can go to."

I told my baby sister this as she was picking out undergraduate schools and law schools. She had already graduated from Northwestern with a degree in engineering, so she knew she was able to get a job. The cost of law school was daunting, and she was weighing the costs of the top schools against other things that she needed.

"I need a car," she told me.

"Look," I said. "Here's the deal. You want a car? If you go to law school, I'll buy you a car." My wife overheard this conversation, but she didn't push back at all. She also knew the importance of relationships and investing in others. Buying this car might seem like an expensive purchase, but I saw it as an incentive for my sister to further her education and an *investment* in my family's life. My wife knew I had taken care of my baby sister for my entire life. My sister accepted the deal. Helping my sister get a car and a law degree was certainly a tremendous investment; she was recently named general counsel of a publicly-traded company. As my experience shows, the best investments are people!

Years later, my sister became a mentor for my daughter Ashley, who also graduated from law school. After graduating, Ashley thrived at the prestigious Kirkland & Ellis law firm. She eventually opened her own practice and today she's the author of multiple books, including *The Law School Hustle,* in which she educates other young people who are interested in taking a similar journey.

Buying that car for my sister was a seed that has provided a harvest for *many* generations. If I were to write the instruction manual for having wealth, it would have to include this story! When you invest in relationships, you will see your investment returned in magnificent ways.

"And he blessed him and said, 'Blessed be Abram by God Most High, Possessor of heaven and earth; and blessed be God Most High, who has delivered your enemies into your hand!' And he gave him a tithe of all." (Genesis 14:19-20 NKJV)

The scripture has a lot to say about wealth, and so do pastors at church. I certainly had a lot to learn once I had money in the bank, but with each lesson, I found myself going back to scripture and to the words I had heard every Sunday.

Some of my earliest memories are about raising the offering at church. Tithing, or giving a tenth of what you reap back to the church, is a practice that can be traced back to Moses and the children of Israel. Tithes aren't required, but many people stick to that practice. I saw people tithing throughout my childhood at the church and I wanted to follow their example.

Working in the mortgage business was a huge turning point in my life. For years, I was able to sit back and listen to scripture without being obligated to act. No one is looking to a child to give up their salary to the church. And although I absorbed as much as I could while I was sitting in the pews, there was always something missing.

Everything came back around to the idea of sowing seeds in good ground. I knew the importance of tithes, so even when I wasn't writing a check directly to the church, I was offering what I had to others.

As I look back and reflect on this lesson of giving, I realize it had been a habit from an early age. I had always wanted to give back to others, whether it was my baby sister or my foster mom, or a friend at school who needed extra help with their homework. Giving was just something that was part of my everyday habits. Even when I didn't have money as a child, I knew that I was doing right by giving what I did have to God. God doesn't need cold, hard cash. As a child, I understood that. Giving back to your community, whether you give your time, labor, or skills, is still giving to God. And giving to God is an act of trust.

When I raised the offering or found ways to help out around the house or the church or the kitchen, I was sowing my trust in God. He had already blessed me with a bounty in the form of my foster home and a warm meal every day. I wanted to continue those practices, sowing more seeds in good ground. It wasn't until many years later that I truly understood the connection between the scripture and my habit of giving back to others; but when it clicked, I realized that I had surrounded myself with people who had the same mindset.

The more I studied wealthy people, like Andy Davis or Leon or Don McNeil or anyone who had money, I started to see a pattern. They gave away their wealth. They paid tithes, sowed seeds, or set up foundations in the community. At the end of the year, the wealthiest people weren't so concerned with how much money they brought in as how much money they gave away. Not everyone did this because they read scripture or were a practicing Christian. I worked with people who belonged to many religions and came from many backgrounds. But as Matthew 5:45

(NKJV) says, *"...for He makes His sun rise on the evil and on the good, and sends rain on the just and on the unjust."* Although I'm a Christian, it doesn't matter who someone worships or whether they worship at all– I believe the law of sowing and reaping applies to everybody.

The more I read books on wealth, mindset, or personal development, the more I confirmed this verse in the scripture. All of these self-help books encouraged readers to give and to treat their wealth like seeds. Failing to do so would have consequences. Sowing corrupt seeds might lead to a harvest of corrupt weeds, to sleepless nights, to barren lands. No matter what you believe or where you make your money, this remains true.

If you don't believe me, believe Warren Buffett. He is one of the five richest people in the world, but that money isn't being drained by an opulent lifestyle. Take a minute to look up where he lives–it's an unassuming house in Omaha, Nebraska. He bought the house in 1958 for $31,500. Talk about modesty! Ninety-nine percent of his wealth, upon his death, is going to charity. He understands that giving to institutions that make a difference in people is the best way to distribute wealth.

When I think about guys like Warren Buffett, I think about the parable of the talents. The story talks about three servants who were given talents (a unit of measurement for precious metals, usually gold or silver).

The first two were able to invest their talents and double their bounty– the third simply buried it and did not see the same return as the first two servants. The parable teaches that God wants a return from every person who claims to be a servant. God takes a little–a little faith, a little trust– and He does a lot with it. No matter what I have, when I give it over to God, he'll increase it. He'll couple it with his strength. He'll couple it with his power, and it'll always end up being more than enough.

"He who is slow to wrath has great understanding, but he who is impulsive exalts folly." (Proverbs 14:29 NKJV)

With faith comes patience. The two are one and the same. Seeds do not grow into a harvest overnight. I learned that once you distribute your wealth strategically, you have to be patient. Wait for the right time to harvest your crops *and* do so without letting your emotions control your actions. Emotions and money don't mix. This final lesson put everything into place for me as I was learning how to manage my money and assets.

Emotions play a huge part in our purchasing decisions if we let them. When my biological father passed away, I was in charge of putting together his funeral. My sisters and I listened to the funeral director as he pitched an elaborate service. I'm sure this man was used to upselling every part of the funeral to emotional families who just wanted the best for their loved ones as they died. There was no such emotion coming from my sisters and me. We wanted to do right by our biological father, but we weren't going to spend any more than we had to.

"Look," I told the director, "I've researched how much these funerals cost. Let's cut the fat out of this thing. We're not going to throw this guy a going-away party where he can't even eat." My sisters and I laughed as we kept negotiating. I'm sure the funeral directors thought we were the meanest kids in the world, but the reality is we weren't going to let our emotions persuade us into spending a fortune on the funeral. When you're conducting business, you have to operate the same way. The idea of wealth and fortune can be emotional, but don't let those daydreams impact your long-term decisions.

I made my biggest mistakes in business when I let my emotions guide me in the wrong direction. By the time I was a father of two, I had a healthy portfolio of stocks that I should have just let sit in the bank. I didn't–I sold many of those shares because I was distracted by the short-term payoff I could get from those sales. I was emotional. If I had just sat on them, I would have been able to use them when they had appreciated even further. If I had waited, maybe I wouldn't have ended up in a place where I couldn't pay the light bill. Impatience led me into the darkness; every stock that I prematurely sold or sold with my emotions ended up costing me money in the long run.

Money doesn't come with instructions, but as I started to write my own manual, I realized just how these "instructions" paralleled life and living as a person of God. Life doesn't come with instructions, either, but what you learn from the Bible and self-help books will directly relate to the experiences that you have. The relationships you form are crucial to the person you become. Giving back to others produces a great return. Patience is key to making it through any darkness in your life. As I endured some of the lowest points in my career and my life, these lessons were put to the test. I thank God for coming out on the other side, with my own version of an instruction manual in hand.

Chapter 8

The Accusation

"A good name is to be chosen rather than great riches, loving favor rather than silver and gold." (Proverbs 22:1 NKJV)

Two officers of the law came in and stood across from my desk. They looked around at everything I had earned in the seven years that I had built Mortgage Lending Corporation. One photo in particular caught their eye.

"Is that Chuck Collins?" one of the officers asked me.

"Yes, sir," I said.

"Are you a Republican, sir?" I laughed. I was neither Republican nor Democrat. Chuck Collins just happened to be one of the first Republican mayors in one of the nearby suburbs. He was also a dear friend of mine that taught me a lot about life.

"Don't distance yourself from wealth," Chuck would always tell me. From what the officers could see that day in my office, I followed that advice. I was far, far away from Robert Taylor. There was no need for me to use food stamps anymore. I had climbed the ladder at Heritage Bank Corporation until I became the first African-American vice president in the organization. Then, I started mortgage lending firms with a group of three partners, and eventually started my own business.

Business was booming. Not only could I afford nice cars and multiple homes and an office in Evergreen Park, but I also had more money to *give away* than ever before in my life. I didn't distance myself from wealth, but I did make sure that everyone else got a piece of it, too.

"Now, what brings you in today, officers?" I asked. Their presence in my office was a surprise that day.

81

"We have been watching quite a few fraudulent transactions closely. Your name has appeared in one."

I was stunned as the officers continued to explain the situation to me. I had no reason to do anything illegal. My involvement in the mortgage business was my ticket *away* from the illegal activities that I had been pressured into committing as a young child in Englewood. I didn't have so much as a speeding ticket on my record.

"Officers," I said, "you must have this wrong. Let me work with you. I can give you whatever information you need to get this all figured out. What paperwork can I send you?"

"You're the one who is mistaken, Williams," one officer told me. "You're involved." He saw how confused I was. Was he talking about a transaction I was involved in personally or a transaction that went through my business? There was no way it could be anything that I touched personally. I didn't need to go around the law to provide for myself and my family. We weren't scrambling for money.

It was only months later that I realized I had put too much trust in a business partner.

"Even if you didn't know about it, you're involved," the officer clarified. "You might have had your head in the sand and let this happen, but you're the man in charge here at Mortgage Lending Corporation, so you have to face the music."

In that one moment, everything fell out from under my feet. I was under arrest.

Everything I had worked for was gone. My name was published in the paper as I was arrested and charged on one count of wire fraud and one count of bank fraud. The dominos started to fall. Who wanted to get a loan from someone who had just been arrested for fraud? I was struggling for work. The economy had already been tanking. I needed to get money together to pay a lawyer. My assets were barely covering the costs of the lifestyle I had before the accusation, and all of a sudden, I couldn't pay the light bill.

I felt like I had nowhere to turn, except to walk toward the glimmer of light and hope that my community, my family, and God were shining on me. When the people in my church heard about what happened, they offered to pull together money for any lawyer I wanted to hire. I almost considered it, too, after I met with a lawyer that Don McNeil knew.

Don knew the former U.S. Attorney, and he knew that it would take someone of his caliber to help me avoid an indictment. You are innocent until proven guilty in this country, but when someone goes up against the federal government, they lose close to 99 percent of the time. I needed this lawyer's honest assessment of my case to help me decide whether or not it was worth the time, effort, and money to go to trial.

The attorney knew Don from high school, but he wanted to learn more about me. "He read the case," Don told me, "but you need to go home and write him a letter about who you are as a man."

I was willing to do so. The letter gave me time to pause and reflect on how this accusation fit into my life's story. I thought about my early days at Carter Temple CME Church, as I learned how to read the Bible. The men in my church taught me not to read the Bible casually, but to look for revelation as I took in these words. Could I do the same as I was taking in this experience? Where could I find revelation?

Even as I wrote the letter, I felt myself gaining confidence in who I was and the journey I was taking. I told the attorney who I was and how I got to where I was. I let him know I was a good man and I couldn't stand to be away from my family. If he could help me, I would be extremely grateful, and I wouldn't squander the opportunity to use this event in my life to help others who might be going through something similar.

We all met a week later at his corner office. As we looked out over the lake, the attorney ate a pasta dish and explained the situation to me.

"Look," he said between bites. "I can take your case. Send me your financial statements. If you can come up with the money, you can go somewhere and play golf. I'll take care of the rest."

This was great news, although my financial statements were only going to reflect what I *had* and what had been taken away as a result of the accusations.

"I've only lost one case," the attorney continued. "And that guy got six months. I can't tell you who this man was, but if you knew his name, you would know that six months was not a whole lot considering his case. Bank fraud comes with possible sentencing of up to thirty years, but there's no way you're getting anything close to that, no matter who represents you. With me, you will be able to walk away without spending a day in jail. I can almost guarantee it."

He leaned in, looking at Don and looking at me. And then he said something I will never forget. "You know that this case came as a direct color of your skin, right? I would have never brought a case like this to the federal government when I was a prosecutor. This is ridiculous, a technical violation at best. You're not a criminal. I will take the case because of who you are and who you have proven to be already. Once you have the money ready for my fees, I'll give you some recommendations for where you can go play golf."

To this day, I believe that he was right. Before the accusations, I had been involved in political activism, and I have reason to believe that my involvement led to an extra eye on any transactions that could fall in the gray areas that businessmen often found themselves in. If I had anticipated this was coming, I could have had money on the side to pay the retainer and go play golf. But I didn't. So instead, I barely had two coins to rub together and a huge case in front of me.

This might come as a shock to you, but it's a reality to many people who have interacted with the country's criminal justice system. The number one crime in America is not bank fraud. It's not murder, it's not the possession of drugs. The number one crime in America is being poor. Whether or not "justice is served" sometimes depends on who has the money and the power to define what justice is in the first place. If I had decided to gather up the money from the people of my church, or if I had made some better choices in building wealth earlier in my career, I could have hired this lawyer and the outcome might have been different. Maybe I wouldn't have had to spend time in prison over what some believed to be a technical violation at worst. But that's not what happened, because despite every honest effort I made to pull myself out of poverty and build wealth for my family and me, the accusations left me impoverished and justice couldn't properly be served.

This realization might have broken other people in my position; the truth that it sheds on the criminal justice system is hard for so many to swallow. I, however, shook hands with the lawyer and left the meeting feeling more confident. I couldn't afford this lawyer, and I knew that. Although the people at my church and some friends of mine offered to help me out, I would have felt just as imprisoned by owing people money as I would if I were to be found guilty. The borrower is a servant to the lender, and I didn't want to be a servant to anyone other than the Lord.

I thanked the lawyer and looked for a more affordable option, but I did so confidently. He was right. This was a case that could be fought in court. I had a chance of an acquittal. What I would do from there, I wasn't sure. But the light was shining brighter on my future, and it gave me the courage to look up and keep walking forward.

"Let no one say when he is tempted, 'I am tempted by God'; for God cannot be tempted by evil, nor does He Himself tempt anyone. But each one is tempted when he is drawn away by his own desires and enticed. Then, when desire has conceived, it gives birth to sin; and sin, when it is

fullgrown, brings forth death. Do not be deceived, my beloved brethren. Every good gift and every perfect gift is from above, and comes down from the Father of lights, with whom there is no variation or shadow of turning. Of His own will He brought us forth by the word of truth, that we might be a kind of firstfruits of His creatures. " (James 1:13-18 NKJV)

As I awaited trial, I had tremendous support from my community. I relied on God to steer me toward the right path. The right path wasn't always obvious at the time. I was tempted. I was desperate, wishing I could get back on my feet. I was considering any carrots dangled in front of me, but I knew that if I listened to Him above anyone else who tried to guide me, I would be on the right track.

In one instance, I received an offer from a young man who had also been a mentee of Wilbert Thomas. For the sake of this story, this man's name was James. James had been around Wilbert's house just as often as I had. He and I bonded over our love of basketball, but he had bigger dreams than hanging around Chicago. He was a singer and a talented singer at that. When I met him, however, his talent only went so far as the "L" trains and a few alleyways of Chicago.

James had money troubles for many years as he struggled to get his big break, and Wilbert and I found different ways to support him. But he also had other struggles. In the middle of a church service once, James pulled me aside with only a quarter to his name. "Every time I make any money," he told me, "it gets taken away from me." He was shaking, and I knew he might be going down a bad path. I didn't get into everything he was going through, but I called Wilbert, and together, the three of us prayed for James. I assured James that the *moment* he was ready to quit was going to be the moment where something great happened for him.

Four weeks later, he got his big break.

In the years that followed, he reached greater and greater heights. James was on top of the world when I was arrested, and when he heard about my struggles, he wanted to return the favors I had given him throughout the years.

"Come on tour, man," he told me. "Be my manager."

Be his manager? I had no experience as a manager. I had only worked as a mortgage banker, and I was working toward a new life in the ministry. Nowhere on my resume was anything that had to do with music or managing a tour. But I considered it when he told me how much he would pay me. "If I have a good year," he told me, "you could be a millionaire. If I don't, you'll still leave the tour with over $700,000 in your pocket."

Well, maybe I could be a manager. This could have been an opportunity to get my family's finances back on track, but I didn't accept right away. I had to pray on it. "Look, James," I told him. "Give me a few days to think about it."

"We leave on Friday," he told me.

I went home that day and started talking to God. Was this an opportunity that I should take? Only God knew. "God," I told Him, "I could have a positive influence on this young man's life. I know he hasn't always followed the path you have laid out for him, but I could help him. Should I go with him, God?"

I received my answer. It was almost like God spoke to me, audibly. "If you go with this man," God told me, "it will be going against my wishes. And you are going to get your butt whooped."

I was shocked! What was God even talking about? I continued praying, asking God what He meant. "Are you sure, God?" I asked, over and over. No response. God said nothing, and He wasn't changing his answer. I made up my mind. I wasn't going to go against that booming voice. God had a reason for giving me such a powerful answer. Who was I to go against Him? The next day, I went back to James and told him that I couldn't accept his offer. "I'm grateful for everything you have offered me, friend, but I'm going to have to say no. Enjoy the tour without me."

"Man, you're crazy!" he told me. "What are you going to do? How are you going to make any money?"

I brushed him off. "A friend offered me a job selling brooms and mops and toilet paper," I joked. James couldn't believe that I was turning the opportunity down, and for a short while, I couldn't believe it either. I trusted God, but I was giving up a lot of money. He must have had a different plan for me, and I had to have faith in that plan.

James got on the bus, started his tour, and two days later was accused of horrific crimes. The accusations he was facing made my two counts of fraud look like nothing. To this day, James' reputation has been dragged through the mud and he may remain a disgraced star for the rest of his life. I don't know how I would have been involved or not involved had I gotten on that bus, but I do know that I am grateful that I listened to God when he told me to walk away.

If you find yourself in a similar situation, I urge you to talk to God. You don't have to be accused of a crime or around any big superstars to receive a powerful answer. Spend a couple of days in the Word before you make any decisions that could take your life in a different direction. The touring lifestyle was not something that I had ever been interested in; I had an idea of what went down on those tour buses and I knew they certainly weren't studying the Bible. But I considered the offer because I was in such a deep depression. I thought I needed the money.

When you're spiraling, there will always be something that will come along to take you further down. That money was tempting me further down. Talk to God before you fall down that spiral. He will make sure that you are instead guided to the light. He will help you look up and get up.

"Be sober, be vigilant; because your adversary the devil walks about like a roaring lion, seeking whom he may devour. Resist him, steadfast in the faith, knowing that the same sufferings are experienced by your brotherhood in the world. But may the God of all grace, who called us to His eternal glory by Christ Jesus, after you have suffered a while, perfect, establish, strengthen, and settle you. To Him be the glory and the dominion forever and ever. Amen." (1 Peter 5:8-11 NKJV)

In the days leading up to the trial, I remained steadfast in my faith. I knew that I could look at my problems like the roaring lion in the Bible. The charges against me came with a potential of thirty years in prison, but I knew I wasn't facing thirty years in prison. I didn't kill anybody. I didn't harm anybody. Sentences like these for white-collar crimes resemble one of many tricks of the enemy; they walk like a roaring lion, but it's important to remember our enemies never *are* roaring lions. They're fake. They're putting on a show in an effort to pull us down mentally and emotionally. I wasn't going to let a fake lion annihilate me.

I saw that God was bigger than my burdens, and I knew my blessings were at hand. The fake lion, the fake teeth, the fake bite of the Devil? It was nowhere near as powerful as God. God was bigger than any adversary I would ever have, whether that was the federal government, the prosecutors in the case, or the systematic injustice that landed me in court in the first place. God was bigger than all of us. Christ defeated death. I was going to draw from that strength and that power, no matter where my journey took me.

Lifting me up during this time was a beautiful community of people present to support me in and out of the courtroom. When I decided to go to trial, Don McNeil was by my side once again to vet my lawyers and give me advice. Two weeks before the trial began, he pulled me aside.

"Keith," he told me, "You have to get another lawyer. This guy has not read your case. He doesn't understand it. Every week, I have been bringing him paperwork to help you out and show your true character.

He isn't listening. He doesn't know how you got tangled up in these charges and he doesn't care. This guy won't read anything."

Don was always by my side to support me. He saw how this lawyer was taking all the money I had and running with it. Don wouldn't stand for it. I got a new lawyer, and the change paid off quickly. While I was originally charged with one count of wire fraud and one count of bank fraud, the wire fraud charge was dropped the day before the trial.

The trial took place over a few weeks, and was presided over by Judge Wayne Andersen. I could give you all the details of the trial, but they might put you to sleep. I will share one story that I think is significant in terms of the odds that are stacked against people fighting the federal government.

Prosecutors aren't as concerned with justice as they are with winning their cases; it's their bread and butter. To win their cases, the best prosecutors create a story that the jury can understand and follow as they make their decision. Within that story is how a crime might have happened, how the defendant was involved, and why the defendant was motivated to commit that crime. Motivation is key to a prosecutor's story.

In my case, the prosecutors tried to paint a picture of me as a greedy man who committed fraud in order to make more money. Any evidence that might be twisted to support that narrative was seen as helpful to the prosecution. Anything that showed me in a more selfless light was something that prosecutors did *not* want in the trial.

So, they did not want my tax returns in the trial.

My defense attorney tried to present my tax returns to the jury. In those returns, anyone could see that greed was not in my nature. I gave away more money than I made. The tax returns obliterated the narrative that the prosecution was trying to paint of me, which is why they didn't want them allowed in the trial. Prosecutors argued that the tax returns would "bias the jury," and they won their argument.

That's right. Despite the tax returns being solid evidence of my financial situation, they were not allowed to be shown to the jury.

Incidents like this remind us of why so many cases brought by the federal government never go to trial. Ninety-five percent of defendants take a plea deal. They believe that it's easier for them to plead guilty and get a reduced sentence than to fight the battle in court. Often, they're right in their beliefs. When you are up against a power that has unlimited resources, you certainly have your work cut out for you. The people in power can tarnish your name, cover up your true story with a false narrative, and send you right to jail. It doesn't always end with a guilty verdict, but often, that's the result. And the only way you're more likely to get an acquittal is if you have the money to afford someone like the first lawyer I talked to before the trial began. Most defense attorneys expect you to take a plea deal. You need someone who has confidence in you; however, that confidence often costs money.

Other than the unfortunate situation with my tax returns, the trial went as expected. The judge listened to my lawyer's arguments and he listened to the few people willing to testify to my character. Not many did; a few people who could have been called to the witness stand were intimidated by the authorities and didn't speak on my behalf. But there was one young lady who did testify. Remember when I worked at the job paying me solely on commission, and the owner's daughter advocated for me to be paid fairly? Her sister, the owner's other daughter, saw the injustices done to me in the courtroom. She testified as an expert witness; she was an underwriter. The prosecutors did not want her on the stand, but she fearlessly answered their questions and spoke to my character. I will never forget what she did that day.

The judge also listened to the prosecutors, who fought *hard* to win the case. And the prosecutors who fought to put me in jail were good at their jobs.

The jury decided to return with a guilty verdict at the end of the trial, but the judge had heard something different in the courtroom. At my sentencing, he addressed me personally. "Keith R. Williams," he said, "I have to tell you something. If I had known the type of person that I had in my courtroom, I would have invited you and your wife over to my house. And I would have told you how to straighten this out." I thought it was strange that he was saying this in front of everyone in the courtroom, but it reminded me of what the former U.S. Attorney had told me all those months before.

Then, he asked me the question: "Do you think you could handle boot camp?"

For those that don't know, "boot camp" is a correctional program that is based on the boot camps in the military. They are much more regimented and physically taxing than a normal prison stay. Every minute of the day is structured for the inmates, and most of those minutes are spent on your feet. These programs are quite intense, but they allow inmates to finish their sentences *much* faster than they would in the typical federal program.

I was looking at six months away from my family if I chose boot camp and twenty-four months away from my family if I didn't choose boot camp. The choice was obvious. Although I was in my forties, a bit older and heavier than the average guy who entered the boot camp program, I had the discipline of a former athlete and the desire to get back to my family sooner. The judge put in a call, and I was on my way to the Federal Intensive Confinement Center in Lewisburg, Pennsylvania.

"Do not be unequally yoked together with unbelievers. For what fellowship has righteousness with lawlessness? And what communion has light with darkness?" (2 Corinthians 6:14 NKJV)

Throughout this entire process, from figuring out how to pay the light bill, to enduring the slanderous picture that the prosecutors tried to paint of me, Valerie was by my side. Remember when I shared the story of Valerie telling me that my seed would sustain us? That happened during the whirlwind of this accusation, trial, and sentencing.

At that moment, when she put her hand on my shoulder, she saw that we were not going in the same direction spiritually. I was being guided by fear, but Valerie was steadfast in her strength. Her words of encouragement allowed me to keep moving forward. Many lose the battle because they give up too quickly, whether that is by taking the plea deal or allowing their fears to take a job that brings them down the wrong path. The war can be won if we recognize the battles as such. God's delays, obstacles, and smaller battles are not His denials, but if we cannot recognize that in our darkest moments, we will be swayed by the enemy. Valerie reminded me to have faith, that victory comes from looking up and taking one more step.

The criminal justice system is not designed for our comfort. Many would even argue that it's designed for our destruction. I see it as a battle– one that you can become victorious over. The process of going through this accusation made me stronger and more mature. I have become more objective in what I read, less judgmental of young men who have been in trouble. Now, I know the battle they are fighting, and I know that without support and faith and God, one can quickly walk down the wrong path.

Once I was out of boot camp, I realized the burdens I carried were not meant to make me bitter but make me better: an advocate for others who might have gone through the same thing. Psalm 30:5 (NKJV) says, *"… weeping may endure for a night, but joy comes in the morning."*

Keep this in mind as you continue to read my story. Weeping endured for many nights as I faced time in boot camp, but I assure you that joy came in the morning.

"For as the rain comes down, and the snow from heaven, and do not return there, but water the earth, and make it bring forth and bud, that it may give seed to the sower and bread to the eater, so shall My word be that goes forth from My mouth; it shall not return to me void, but it shall accomplish what I please, and it shall prosper in the thing for which I sent it." (Isaiah 55:10-11 NKJV)

Years after my time in boot camp was long behind me, I was at a restaurant in downtown Chicago, getting ready to have some breakfast. Who did I see sitting across the room but Judge Andersen. I had to say hello. "Judge Andersen?" I said.

"Keith R. Williams." I thought it was so strange that he remembered my name, but I was delighted. I gave him a big bear hug.

The judge looked at me said, "Out of all the cases I have tried in my career, yours is the one that never left my mind. How are you doing?"

"I'm doing just fine, Judge."

"I'm so sorry you had to go through that," he told me. But I held up my hand.

"Your Honor, sometimes bad things happen to good people for good reasons. At the end of the day, I just want you to know that I appreciate you."

A few years after that, Judge Andersen went to speak at a class at Northwestern Law School. One of the students approached him after the class. He could tell that she was one of the top students, taking careful notes during his presentation.

"Have you ever met a Keith R. Williams?" she asked him.

"Yes, I have."

"Well," she said, "that's my dad." Ashley, my oldest daughter, had fallen in love with the law. And her time at Northwestern was just the beginning of her successful law career. Isn't it nice when these things come full circle?

Chapter 9

The Dungeon

"Now no chastening seems to be joyful for the present, but painful; nevertheless, afterward it yields the peaceable fruit of righteousness to those who have been trained by it." (Hebrews 12:11 NKJV)

Before everything came full circle, I had to face boot camp. You don't need me to tell you that the weeks leading up to my sentence were psychologically draining. When you are going through a federal indictment, you take on a mental, emotional, and financial burden that no one can anticipate. I often refer to this time in my life as "the dungeon," not just because I was in a prison with high walls and next to no freedom, but because my mind felt like a dungeon, too. I was trapped by the fear of what was to come and the frustration that I could not provide for my family.

In times like this, when you feel as though you are existing in a dungeon, people might tell you to just focus on the day ahead. *Just get through the day,* they tell you *and worry about tomorrow later.*

I was so drained that "getting through the day" was too overwhelming. I had to just focus on getting through the next sixty seconds. My wife was so crucial in helping me see the light and make each sixty seconds an opportunity to push forward. Hearing her voice in my head, telling me that "your seed will sustain us," was just what I needed to feel better in my darkest moments.

As I said goodbye to her on my way to the Federal Intensive Confinement Center, I knew that I would tap into that faith and strength to get me through the next sixty seconds, and the sixty seconds after that, and the sixty seconds after that.

Off I went, on a plane to Pennsylvania, to turn myself in. A cab was waiting at the airport when I arrived.

"Where are you going?" the cab driver asked.

"The Federal Intensive Confinement Center," I told him. I'm sure he told his family about the ride when he got home that night.

The taxi took me through the gates to where a guard was posted. "I'm here for boot camp," I told him. I just had to get through the next sixty seconds, but I was sure not going to spend that next sixty seconds wearing handcuffs. I also resolved that I was never going to put on a pair of handcuffs again. The guard looked at me as the cab drove off. I could feel, in the anticipation of what was going to happen next, that I was truly living the darkest moment of my life.

"Look," the guard said. "I'm supposed to put some cuffs on you and drive you over to get you checked in." He paused. "I'm not going to do that. Can you just get in the back of the car?" No handcuffs for me. I should have felt great relief at that moment, but in that relief, I could only ask myself the question, "What did I do to deserve this?"

During the check-in process, I got a gruff speech from one of the guards, who I'll call Ronald. Ronald was white with a shiny bald head. You knew you were not supposed to look in his eyes from the moment you met him, but he took pleasure in telling you that rule anyway. (Yes, that was a rule in boot camp. Of all the rules, I think that one should change.)

"Listen here, boys," he started. "This is the Lewisburg Intensive Confinement Center. And it's the Hate Capital of the World, according to the FBI. All those hate groups you hear about on the news? Yeah, those guys are here. Those guys *work* here. Welcome to the beginning of your incarceration. Now, how do you want your hair cut?"

Everything that Ronald and the staff at the prison did was intended to intimidate the inmates. I saw through it faster than some, because I knew whatever they tried to do wasn't going to be anything worse than what I had seen on the streets. I knew they were going to try to trick me, so when they asked me how I wanted my hair cut, I told them to shave it all off. They were going to anyway. Guys behind me told them to just take a little off the top and, the next thing they knew, the razor was shaving right down the middle. Cruel stuff.

Every minute of the day was scheduled. No inmate had any choices. We had to ask for permission to go to the bathroom or speak to the guards. Looking back, despite some of the harsher rules, I still have positive things to say about those six months. The judge was not sure that I was going to be able to handle boot camp because I was about fifty pounds overweight. I sure got myself back into shape. We were on our feet more often than not. That fifty pounds disappeared and I was able to reset my approach to eating healthy and working out by the time I got out.

Over time, I could see a positive transformation taking place in many of the inmates who were going through the boot camp program. I wasn't sharing a cell with the toughest guys I had ever met. Everyone in prison with me had either committed low-level drug crimes or had lawyers like mine that advocated for the program so we could get back to our families faster. I only saw two fights in prison because the rules placed on us and the discipline required of us were so intense.

Every activity scheduled for us, every minute of the day, was a part of a larger goal. We would have to repeat this goal to the guards frequently: "I'm here to change and become a progressively better person." Sometimes we would have to rattle off a whole speech based on this phrase, but other times we would just have to repeat these few words, over and over, until they stuck. I didn't go into prison because I was a bad person. I was caught in a technical violation and I didn't have the money to see justice served. But the discipline that I sharpened during that time helped me fortify my faith in Christ. I became a progressively better person.

The biggest challenge in the kingdom of God, in my opinion, is discipline. I'm talking about more than just getting up when your alarm clock goes off. Discipline takes years, often years of hardship, to develop. But it pays off. Who were the people closest to Jesus? The disciples. The word "disciples" comes from the word "discipline," and that is no coincidence. Discipline, for many, requires a change, but it's a good change that helps you become a progressively better person.

"By the rivers of Babylon, there we sat down, yea, we wept when we remembered Zion. We hung our harps upon the willows in the midst of it. For there those who carried us away captive asked of us a song, and those who plundered us requested mirth, saying, 'Sing us one of the songs of Zion!' How shall we sing the Lord's song in a foreign land? If I forget you, O Jerusalem, let my right hand forget its skill! If I do not remember you, let my tongue cling to the roof of my mouth–if I do not exalt Jerusalem above my chief joy." (Psalm 137:1-7 NKJV)

I'm not trying to say that I enjoyed those six months. The schedule was demeaning. We had very few moments to ourselves. When we had those moments, I found ways to steal away and peek at the Word of God. God got me through that time in the dungeon. In the moments where I consulted the scriptures, I felt like I was back at the church of my childhood once again, listening to my pastor read the stories for the first time. *If I could just learn one new thing,* I told myself, *I can get through the next sixty seconds.*

I thought about Psalm 137. The children of Israel were enslaved by their captors. They were mocked for singing the songs of Zion. Yet, they still found the strength and the time to praise God. In reflecting on that story, I knew I had to do the same.

With that in mind, I wasn't only thinking about getting through the next sixty seconds. I wanted to use that sixty seconds to praise God. I started singing old-fashioned songs like "At The Cross":

"At the cross, at the cross,

Where I first saw the light

And the burden of my heart rolled away, rolled away

It was there by faith I received my sight

And now I am happy all the day!"

The words helped me feel a joy that I hadn't been able to feel since the accusation. I thought about the people at my church that would sing songs like this. I thought about Mom and Wilbert Thomas and all the people who welcomed me into the church. I thought about all of the days where I *was* happy all the day: the night I met my wife, the day we went ring shopping, our wedding, the births of our two children. Through these songs and this praise, I concluded that even if I didn't live to see another day, God had still been good to me. He was kind to me. He was merciful. I knew that, no matter what the next sixty seconds would bring, I could lean on the never-ending power of His Word.

The power of the Word of God shall endure forever.

I believe that we determine our outcome, despite where we are, by three things. We determine our outcome by *what we say.* We determine our outcome by *what we believe.* And we determine our outcome by *standing on the covenantal promises* that are written in His Word. I don't care what you look like, where you came from, or what you do for a living. Your outcome will be based on how you speak the Word and how you advance the Word by faith right now. How are you going to spend the next sixty seconds? Tests of faith don't wait.

Mark 11:24 (NKJV) says, *"Therefore I say to you, whatever things you ask when you pray, believe that you receive them, and you will have them."* When we believe it, we will receive it. I believed before I entered the dungeon that was the Federal Intensive Confinement Center, that I was never going to wear handcuffs again. I believed I was going to make it through boot camp and prosper once again. I believed that I was going to dedicate the rest of my life to the Word of God. And because I believed it, that is what I received.

Chapter 10

Resurrection Sunday

"'...for I was hungry and you gave Me food; I was thirsty and you gave Me drink; I was a stranger and you took Me in; I was naked and you clothed Me; I was sick and you visited Me; I was in prison and you came to Me.' Then the righteous will answer Him, saying, 'Lord, when did we see You hungry and feed You, or thirsty and give You drink? When did we see You a stranger and take You in, or naked and clothe You? Or when did we see You sick, or in prison, and come to You?' And the King will answer and say to them, 'Assuredly, I say to you, inasmuch as you did it to one of the least of these My brethren, you did it to Me.'" (Matthew 25:35-40 NKJV)

I nmates in federal facilities are entitled to two religious services a week.

A lot of the men in the prison would attend just so they could sit down for an hour. They let the Word of God roll right over their heads, and if they were lucky, they would grab a few minutes of sleep.

Now, it shouldn't surprise you that I wasn't sleeping through these services. I was engaged. Before I had gone to the dungeon I had been working as an assistant pastor and earned a license to preach through the Methodist Church. When I entered boot camp, I was just another inmate in the seats. An outside group came to conduct the religious services every week, and while some of the inmates continued to nod off, I asked questions. I wanted to continue the discussion. The organization that held the services were believers, but they didn't always go by the same doctrine that was taught at the Methodist Church.

"Tell me where you find this story in the Bible," I would ask them. "Show me." This always started a debate. The group would point to one passage and give their interpretation. I would share what it meant. Over and over again, week after week, we would get into debates. All of these debates boiled down to one thing: they believed in a private interpretation of the Word of God. I didn't. While I was happy to continue debating, the group was not as amused by my questions. With that difference between us, the organization stopped coming to the facility!

A lot of the inmates were not happy about this. When were they going to sit down for an hour? So, they turned to me. "Would you be interested in holding the service?" At first, I hesitated. I just wanted to focus all my energy on getting home to my family. But this was an opportunity to reach people that I wouldn't be able to reach otherwise. When else was I going to sit down, with men of color and men in these vicious hate groups, and come to a common understanding? We were all from different backgrounds, and because I had grown up in some of the roughest neighborhoods of Chicago, none of the guys intimidated me much. "Sure," I said. "I'll lead the service."

"Give, and it will be given to you; good measure, pressed down, shaken together, and running over will be put into your bosom. For with the same measure that you use, it will be measured back to you." (Luke 6:38 NKJV)

I think about this passage often when reflecting on the services I led at boot camp. When the scripture says, "Shall men give into your bosoms," it doesn't specify "white men" or "Black men" or "Italians" or "Irishmen." The scripture just says "men." When we allow ourselves to look to the Word, the Word will show us that God's best exists in all people, and that includes people who have been led astray or made mistakes or were raised to think differently than ourselves.

When I was in boot camp, I witnessed God's best being revealed in men. White men, Black men, you name it. We rarely get the opportunity to see this type of meshing "outside." Our society is telling a different story: one where people segregate themselves, keep to their own, and fail to talk to each other. Religion is not immune to this. Sunday morning is typically the most segregated time in the country. A Black church may be right across the street from a white church, and although we're reading the same Word and serving the same God, we're not mingling with each other. Boot camp forced men of different races to come together, and although it was not under ideal terms, we still came together. In those services, everyone did come together, loving and confessing the same Christ.

Obviously, this didn't happen overnight. Tensions were high. Before I started holding services, I had gotten myself into a little beef with an Italian man and an Irish man who called one of the young Black men "boy." I didn't know if these men understood the implications and racist history of calling a Black man "boy," so I gently confronted them. They had already been having a conversation, and I added my two cents. I didn't curse, didn't point fingers, didn't accuse anyone of anything. I knew how heated things could get, but I also knew how quickly an act of violence or riot could result in guys going to another facility and serving the rest of their term. These men didn't attack me, but they still had a beef with me. They threatened me and called me names. I didn't care. I was from one of the roughest neighborhoods in Chicago. I had already heard all the stuff they were throwing at me. They weren't going to risk having to go to another facility, so I let them say what they said and moved on.

Soon after that incident, all three of us witnessed a miracle that changed our relationship. I believe that this miracle brought them to Christ. The miracle happened in the late hours of the night. I'm not sure where the guards were at the time, but we were all awakened by the sound of chaos. One of the inmates, a Haitian man, had stopped breathing. He had clearly been experiencing some kind of trauma, but to this day I don't know what led him to this moment.

Immediately, everyone around this man jumped out of their bunks to help. The man wasn't responsive. The guards were nowhere to be found. A white man who was close by took it upon himself to give him mouth-to-mouth. No response. I sat at the man's feet and prayed.

"Lord," I said, "I believe that it is your will that he lives."

I said it again. "Lord, I believe that it is your will that he lives."

A third time: "Lord, I believe that it is your will that he lives."

After the third time, the man popped up. He was breathing. He was alive! Mouth-to-mouth and CPR hadn't worked, but the Lord saved him. I looked around at all the men who had witnessed the situation. The Italian and the Irish guy who had threatened me earlier were there to watch. They were moved–I saw it in their eyes. And from that moment on, a revival took place in the boot camp that I believe saved these men, among many others, in more ways than one.

A few weeks later, I held a service. I asked all of the inmates, "Is there anybody that wants to be saved? Who wants to be sure about their salvation?"

Whose hand did I see but that Italian kid? He came up to the front of the room, hand in the air, asking to be saved. Whether it was the service, the miracle that we had witnessed, or the Holy Spirit, I don't know. But he was in a state that was unlike anything I had seen from him throughout our time in boot camp. He was crying like a baby. Tears were streaming down his face. Upon the sight of him, I was crying, too. Everybody was crying! Together, we all prayed and asked God to bless him. This kid was confessing Christ as the Lord and Savior of his life.

The Irish guy joined him. He was also in his forties, and I knew he was very unfamiliar with services like mine. "I don't like what I'm feeling," he told me. He was also crying. "I don't like the salvation stuff." But he felt moved to stand up at the front of the room that day. Weeks before, he and this Italian guy and I were at odds with each other. Christ brought us together.

"You might think you don't like how you're feeling right now," I told him, "but you will. The power of God can't be quantified. I can't explain it. It's too powerful. The Word says, 'Therefore, if anyone is in Christ, he is a new creation; old things have passed away; behold, all things have become new.' This is what rebirth is all about, man. It's not about my skin color, your skin color, you, me, all of them, any of that. All that matters is, if we love God, we have to find a way to love each other. It's that simple."

And with that, this inmate confessed Christ.

"For since by man came death, by Man also came the resurrection of the dead. For as in Adam all die, even so in Christ all shall be made alive." (1 Corinthians 15:21-23 NKJV)

I was in boot camp for Resurrection Sunday, also known as Easter. I was looking forward to that day, as I knew my wife was coming to visit me after lunchtime. Valerie found a way to visit me frequently, fixing up her old car (we had to sell the Mercedes) and driving from Chicago to

Lewisburg. On that day, we planned to celebrate the Lord and all that he had given us.

The inmates and I ate lunch then walked back in formation toward the barracks. Ronald was leading the way, but one of the inmates had the nerve to say something or do something to offend him. I don't even remember what he did, but I remember Ronald's hot temper.

"Okay, boys," the guard told us, "here's the deal. I'm going to cancel your Easter Sunday. No visitations!"

I had the choice to feel devastated, but I chose instead to feel empowered. No one was going to mess with Resurrection Sunday. I knew how much of a risk it was to talk back to Ronald in boot camp. If the guards don't approve you at the end of your six months, you have to go to a federal facility and do 85 percent of your sentence. They can kick you out at any time, for any reason. Saying anything and doing anything was a huge risk, but it was a risk I was moved to take at that moment. I was going to be bold in my righteousness.

I got out of formation, which was already a risk, and marched alongside Ronald. Without looking him in the eye, I said, "Permission to speak, sir."

The cuss words started flying out of Ronald's mouth, but he let me speak.

"Sir," I said, "America is predominantly a Judeo-Christian society. Resurrection Sunday is the holiest time of the year for a believer. I wish you would reconsider canceling it."

I didn't tell him my wife was visiting.

The cuss words kept flying out of Ronald's mouth! And then he told me, "You meet me at my office, Williams, and I'm going to throw you out of here. I'm going to see how you really feel about, what did you call it? Resurrection Sunday? I'll see how you feel about it while you're serving the rest of your time. Back in line!"

On the way back to my spot in the formation, a lot of inmates shared their thoughts: "Williams, we're praying for you." "Williams, I think you're going to be alright." "Williams, you should have shut your freaking mouth back there."

I didn't. I felt like Daniel in the lion's den. Like Shadrach, Meshach, and Abednego in the fiery furnace. For the next sixty seconds, I was going to be brave for the celebration of the Resurrection. I was confident in what was coming next, even if all of the other inmates weren't. Praising the Lord on Resurrection Sunday with my wife was worth the risk.

I went into Ronald's office and sat down. The cuss words started flying toward me once again, and I just politely listened. On and on: "If you're so freaking righteous, how did you end up in this place? I'm going to throw you out of here!" I waited for him to finish his rant.

"Permission to speak, sir," I said.

"Okay, let me hear it."

"Well, sir, as I understand it I'm here to progressively change and become a better person. And sir, I would just ask you to look at the scripture. I believe that you have some knowledge of the Bible. If you look at the scripture, you can take a look at the disciples. All of them had causes against the government. All of them caught cases. Look at Daniel, look at Shadrach, Meshach, and Abednego. All of those people were incarcerated. Sir, you can look at Joseph, who was entangled based on something he didn't do. He was incarcerated, too. Sir, look at the Apostle Paul! He was caught up in prisons, in chains."

108

I went on and on, listing all of the men of the Bible who had been incarcerated. In moments of despair in the dungeon, these men had brought me solace. Now, they were empowering me, and I could tell that their stories were reaching into Ronald's heart, too.

"Look it over, please, sir." I hadn't looked up at Ronald since I started talking, but I could hear his reaction. Ronald was crying. He was sobbing like a baby!

"Williams," he said through his teeth, "don't you look at me." He was sniffling. "You better not look at me, Williams!" The Holy Spirit was moving him, I just knew it. I stayed quiet, letting the Word of God run through him. Patiently, I waited for him to pull himself together.

After he wiped his tears, Ronald spoke again. "Let me tell you something, Williams. My bark is always going to be bigger than my bite. Before today, Satan had gotten control of me, but somehow in this room, I feel the presence of the Lord."

I did, too. I felt chills as Ronald had fought the Devil in that office and accepted the Lord.

"What did you call today, Williams? Resurrection Sunday. I'm not canceling your Resurrection Sunday. But if you tell *anyone* about what you saw in this office, I'm going to get you."

Back at my barracks, all of the inmates were curious. "What happened, Williams?" "Are you leaving?" "What did Ronald say?" All I told them was, "It's going to be okay. It's going to be okay." And we had a beautiful Resurrection Sunday celebration that afternoon.

From there on out, Ronald and I formed a bond. I wouldn't say we were ever best friends, but we talked more openly about the Word of God, compassion, and forgiveness. There were plenty of times when

Ronald would want to throw a young guy out of boot camp for mouthing off or screwing around. He would ask me what I thought, and I would say the same thing.

"Sir, I know what you're thinking. I know this guy messed up. You could easily throw him out of here and make him go do the rest of his time in a regular federal penitentiary. But why don't you just think about it overnight?"

The next day, Ronald would always come back in a calmer mood. He told me he went home to his family and spent time with his children. His children were wise, and they always spoke to him about forgiveness.

"So, I'll give this guy another chance," Ronald would tell me. "But if he blows it again, I'm going to throw him out of here!"

"Sounds good," I would tell him. "Sounds good."

Chapter 11

Stepping Stones

"You have heard that it was said, 'You shall love your neighbor and hate your enemy.' But I say to you, love your enemies, bless those who curse you, do good to those who hate you, and pray for those who spitefully use you and persecute you, that you may be sons of your Father in heaven; for He makes His sun rise on the evil and on the good, and sends rain on the just and on the unjust. For if you love those who love you, what reward have you? Do not even the tax collectors do the same? And if you greet your brethren only, what do you do more than others? Do not even the tax collectors do so? Therefore you shall be perfect, just as your Father in heaven is perfect."
(Matthew 5:43-48 NKJV)

The most challenging interaction between me and Ronald came at the end of my time in boot camp. He called me into my office one day
and asked me about a man that I'll call Moose.

"You know Moose?" he asked me.

I knew Moose, but I tried to avoid Moose. He belonged to one of the many hate groups that Ronald had referenced at the start of my time at boot camp. Was Moose a skinhead? I never asked, and I didn't intend to ask. I kept out of his way and he kept out of mine.

Ronald called me into his office because Moose was sick. He was bitten by a spider and the bite had turned into a nasty infection. Nothing they had tried at the facility was helping, and time was running out for Moose to stay in boot camp. If you get sick or injured during your time, you have to go back to a regular prison and carry out your full sentence.

For some guys, getting sick meant they had to spend another year, ten years, or even twenty years behind bars. Moose was heading down that road.

"Williams," Ronald told me, "ever since you've been doing Bible studies, we've got a lot of spiritual activity going on around here."

"Well, thank you, sir. Glad to spread the Word of God."

"I'm going to need you to direct that spirituality to Moose."

"What?" Moose wasn't involved in any of the spiritual activities. He hadn't confessed Christ and he preferred to stand an extra hour instead of joining us in prayer.

"He's not doing so well, Williams. We've given him antibiotics, cleaned him up, but he might still have to leave boot camp. The man needs a miracle. Will you pray for him?"

Would I? The answer wasn't so simple. With anyone else, I would have said yes immediately. But Moose was not the first person on your list that you would want to receive a miracle. I questioned whether he would ever offer me the same grace. This was a huge test of my faith, but so was my whole time in boot camp. I told Ronald I would do what I could and went back to my cell.

"Lord, you gotta help me here," I prayed. Matthew's words on praying for your enemies washed over me, and I prayed. I prayed for Moose to get better. I prayed as I would pray for someone who I loved very dearly because God encouraged me to keep praying. Within twenty-four hours the infection cleared in Moose's body and he was allowed to continue at boot camp. He would be able to carry out a shorter sentence.

When I heard this news, I felt better than I did when I started praying for Moose. I felt relieved! It took a lot of strength for me to ask God to heal this man, a man who I believed wouldn't bat an eye if I was shipped off to a regular prison or even lost my life. But God told me to keep praying for him, and I did. After passing that test, Moose was healed.

I didn't tell Moose the next day that my prayers had healed him. I believe he knew that something miraculous had happened to him; however, I still had to share something with Moose. This was not the end of my test. In my prayers, God gave me a specific message that *I* needed to share with Moose.

"Tell him," the Lord told me, "that one day, he is going to preach the gospel. Everything that this man has done in the past has been a stepping stone for what he is going to do in the future."

The Lord had more tests in store for me. I didn't want to give Moose this message. I didn't want to say anything to him! If Moose and I had never spoken again, I would have continued to live a prosperous life. That wasn't God's plan. The first chance I got, I went up to Moose, let him know that I was glad he was feeling better and told him the message the Lord wanted me to give to him.

Now, Moose didn't become a pastor as fast as he healed from his spider bite. He didn't take over my spot at Bible study. We didn't become friends and we pretty much avoided each other for the rest of our sentences. But we were released at the same time, and something amazing happened. The day I left boot camp, a few members of the church picked me up. A few members of Moose's family picked him up, too. All of us ended up at the same rest stop on the way to our respective homes.

Our two groups couldn't look more different: a group of church-going Black folks and a bunch of white folks who *all* looked like they belonged to a hate group or two. When Moose saw me at the rest stop,

113

however, he didn't hide amongst his hillbilly cousins. He called me over and introduced me to his family. A few members of the church might have raised an eyebrow, but they were amazed at what Moose told his family.

"You see this guy right here?" Moose asked. "He said that I'm going to one day preach the gospel. Can you believe it?"

Moose's group looked at my group and then looked back at Moose. They shook their heads. They couldn't believe it.

"Well, listen here," Moose told them, "I believe him. I believe I'm going to preach the gospel one day."

That was the last time that I ever saw Moose. Who knows what he is doing now, but I believe that moment stuck with him as it stuck with me. Praying for him was one of the biggest hurdles I had to jump in boot camp. I continue to remember him when I'm attending protests and working in social action and standing toe-to-toe with people like Moose.

I know a lot of people who prefer to be around people of their own race, and I'm talking about white, Black, Asian, everyone. But I believe that this approach is close-minded. It's the kind of mindset that got me in prison in the first place. When you make a fist, nothing can come in and nothing can come out. Alienating ourselves gets us nowhere. We all lose. We have to come together and see God's best in each other.

I certainly don't walk around in different neighborhoods looking for skinheads to befriend, and I'm not going to do anything foolish to reach out and help someone who is different from myself. But I am not going to alienate myself from people just because they don't look like me or didn't grow up where I grew up. My relationships are strategic. How can I learn from someone? How can I help them? How can they help me? I do all of this, knowing that God would encourage me to pray for them.

"Bear one another's burdens, and so fulfill the law of Christ." (Galatians 6:2 NKJV)

The importance of strategic relationships, a lesson I learned way back in my early days as a mortgage lender, allowed me to not only establish a career way back when but also helped me get back on my feet after I went through hard times.

My fight wasn't over when I arrived back home, and I wasn't fully out of the dungeon. I had to get back on my feet and start making a living once again. I could have easily gone back to the mortgage business, but I refused. I didn't want to go back. The time I experienced in the dungeon, from the moment I was accused of fraud to the moment I was released and started paying restitution, was enough for me to never want to reenter my old career. I had to try something new.

And when I say I could have easily done it, I'm not bluffing. The bank fraud charge was no more than a technical violation. My license wasn't even revoked. Several people, upon my arrival in Chicago, were ready to offer me a six-figure job the moment I arrived back home. One person offered me a position as a trainer at their mortgage company. Another person told me I was going to be making $75,000 minimum. I turned all of these jobs down.

Instead, I started working in construction. You read that right! My pastor at the time had a construction company doing government work. I was making a fraction of what I had been making before the accusation, but I didn't mind. I was working, I was moving forward with my life, and I was surrounded by a lot of men from the church. These were men like Wilbert Thomas who could set an example for how I wanted to live in this new chapter.

A few months into this job, Leon gave me a call. I should say that *Uncle* Leon gave me a call. By the time I was out of boot camp, Leon had been in my life and my family's life so much that my kids called him Uncle. He was one of the people that truly showed me and my children the importance of strategic relationships, as well as teaching me a bit about humility and frugality. Once again, Leon wanted to meet with me to talk about a problem he had in his lending portfolio. The property was on the South Side, and he knew that I knew the area better than anyone else.

"No problem," I told him. "Why don't you meet with me at the construction site where I'm working?" Leon agreed, and I couldn't help but chuckle to myself. At the time, I was working in one of the toughest neighborhoods on the West Side of Chicago. This might have been one of the toughest neighborhoods in the whole country. As I ate my lunch on the vacant lot where we were building, I could see gunfights and all sorts of trouble going on. I had just spent six months in a federal correctional facility, but *this* felt like a movie.

Leon was shocked when he pulled up to meet me. He took one look around the place and said, "You know I have resources, right?" It was not Leon's way to come right out and tell me he could loan me the money to get out of working here, but that's what he meant. I just told him to tell me what problem he was facing with his property.

He did, and his problems weren't that substantial. I told him that I could help him fix the problem in ninety days.

This answer satisfied Leon, but he remained uneasy about where I was working. "Do you remember where I live?" he asked me. "Do you know what resources I have? We've done business together. You're a good guy. What are you doing over here?"

"Look, Leon, I just need to be in a safe place right now." Leon looked down at my lunch. I was eating peanut butter sandwiches every day just to save a few bucks. The work boots on my feet were boots that my pastor's father had given me after a few weeks on the job. I didn't mind this step away from my previous life of wealth, because I knew that a blessing would come later to me and my family. I always had faith in that blessing. I just had no idea that that day, over my peanut butter sandwich in one of the roughest neighborhoods in Chicago, Leon would be that blessing.

"You're solving a problem for me," Leon said. "So, I've got a deal for you. If this strategy works out the way you say it will, I'm going to make you my business partner. You won't have to work in the mortgage business, but you will be able to make some money in real estate and have a better lunch than this peanut butter sandwich. For our first deal, you won't have to put anything down. Later on, you'll need to invest money, but you'll have money in the bank that you can invest. What do you want to do, Keith?"

I thought about Leon's offer for a minute. Mortgage lending was no longer in my future, but I had gained a liking for real estate before I had ever decided to walk away from lending. Working on homes with my bare hands gave me a further appreciation for the business, too.

"Well, Leon," I told him. "Let's see how this strategy works out. I'm interested."

The strategy worked, and I was back on my feet, providing for my family while working in the real estate business.

"...not forsaking the assembling of ourselves together, as is the manner of some, but exhorting one another, and so much the more as you see the day approaching. (Hebrews 10:25 NKJV)

I made the right decision by getting into real estate with Leon. One of the investments I made with Leon came back tenfold. I had money to pay the bills, pay restitution, and enjoy some leftover cash for spending. When this happened, the first person I wanted to talk to was John.

John was one of the three business partners I had before I went off on my own. After the accusation, John stood by my side. I knew he would: we had spent so many years together in the mortgage business. We trusted each other, even when that trust was shaken. John stood up for me even in times when others turned their backs on me.

Shortly after the accusation, John had lunch with a guy who had worked for me at one point. Let's call this guy Craig. Craig didn't know that I had a business relationship with John. He didn't know how close we were. But he knew John, and they had many lunches together. One day, this guy asked John, "Do you know Keith Williams? Man, that guy is in a lot of trouble. He's not going to come out on the other side." John just listened as Craig mouthed off. This was soon after I had been accused, and John didn't even know that I was in trouble!

After Craig had run his mouth for way too long, John stopped him. "Yes, I know Keith. And guess what? Keith is my friend. I didn't know he was having trouble. So, if you'll excuse me, I'm going to make a call to Keith Williams and see how he's doing." John left the table and he set up a lunch for the two of us. And at that lunch, he loaned me $75,000.

He was the first person I wanted to pay back after I started making money again. I paid him the loan in full. John looked at me, money in hand, and said, "Keith, I didn't know if you were ever going to be able to pay me back. I'm certainly happy you could. But just know that I wasn't doing it to gain anything or even to get that money back. We're friends. Friends take care of friends."

John has always been a blessing in my life, just like Leon has been a blessing in my life. When I think about men like John and Leon, who were able to extend their hand and be a blessing, I am reminded that God uses people. God can bless you any way that He wants to. He could have showered me with $75,000 at any time. If He can rain manna from the Heavens, He could have found a way to help me get back on my feet after boot camp. If He gave the children of Israel water by striking a stone, He could have done anything to help me pay back those that I owed. The thing about God is that He doesn't always work like that. God gives you the revelation of His Holy Spirit. He gives you a body of believers that will stand with you in times of trouble. He uses people, whether or not you see Him using them.

I have joined myself to a body of people that believe in me. Those people may, at times, have looked like the enemy. Whereas some people may alienate themselves from others based on the color of their skin or their background, I know that God puts these people in front of us as an opportunity. I see them the way that God presents them to me.

Not every person is going to be a blessing in the way that John and Leon have been. Some people will be put in your path the way that Moose was put in my path. Moose was a test of faith. In his own way, he was a stepping stone to where I am today, because he was a reminder that without a community of people who believe and share in the Word of God, we can easily become lost.

Time and time again, the people in my life have proven to be stepping stones to where I am today. In this revelation, after time in the dungeon and time at the height of my career, I understand that I have the power to be this stepping stone for others, and I can help others join themselves to a body of people that believe in them, too.

Chapter 12

Recompense

"So I will restore to you the years that the swarming locust has eaten, the crawling locust, the consuming locust, and the chewing locust, my great army which I sent among you." (Joel 2:25 NKJV)

If you have been wronged, there will be a time in your life where that wrong will be reconciled and you will get more than what your trouble took away. You won't just get back what you lost; you will get everything back multiplied. In my life, these multiples have come in the form of miracles. The miracles that I have experienced, before and after my time in the dungeon, have come directly from God.

One of these miracles started with a call from the West Side of Chicago. It was a Sunday evening and my wife and I had just arrived home from church.

"Is this Keith Williams?" the man on the phone said.

"Yes, who's calling?"

"I'm a private investigator," he told me. "Your sister has hired me. I believe you have a sister that you don't know about."

When I heard this, I thought my cousins on the West Side were pulling a prank on me! It was something that they would do. I wrote down this "private investigator's" number and called my older sister. "This guy is calling me and telling me that we might have another sister," I told her. "Can you believe that? What are our cousins up to now?"

"Actually," she told me, "that sounds about right. Mamie had a child that she put up for adoption." Mamie was what we called our birth mother. My sister and I talked about Mamie here and there, but in all the years that she was alive she *never* mentioned to me that she had another child!

"Don't you think this is something that you might have mentioned to me?" I asked my sister. We laughed and I let her know that I'd arrange a meeting for all of us.

I called the private investigator back and spoke a little more warmly to him now that I knew he wasn't a prank call from my cousins.

"Do you want to meet your sister?" he asked. I said yes, and we set up a place to meet. The place where I met my oldest sister was a restaurant called Captain Hard Times, and it was located right down the street from the Carter Temple CME Church. Driving down to the neighborhood with my two sisters and my wife felt like old times. The son of the man who owned the restaurant and I even grew up going to church together. We pulled into a parking space and caught sight of a woman walking across the street. I nudged my wife.

"That's my sister." I knew it immediately, and I was right.

We had a beautiful meal together. As it turns out, my sister grew up two blocks from our church. She attended Girl Scout meetings at our church, too. All our lives, we walked right past each other and didn't know the bond that we shared.

I immediately knew that this woman was my sister, but once we ordered our food at Captain Hard Times, there was no denying we had the same genes. My whole life, I've tried foods from all over the world.

I've loved Greek food, Italian food, kosher food, everything. Out of all my friends, I've always had the most eclectic food tastes. (Just no bananas.) Once my sister and I ordered our food, we realized we had the same palette, exploring and loving food all types of food.

Since I experienced the miracle of meeting my oldest sister, we've traveled together and I've learned all about her life growing up, working for the airlines, and retiring. My older sister and I were not able to grow up together as a family, but we have been blessed over and over again by meeting each other and getting to know each other's family. I've gained nieces and grandnieces as a result of meeting her. Meanwhile, my baby sister, my daughter, and one of my oldest sister daughter's and I all live within five miles of each other. Talk about blessings multiplied! Her finding us was truly a miracle.

"Give to everyone who asks of you. And from him who takes away your goods do not ask them back." (Luke 6:30 NKJV)

In the past few years, I've been "accused" of something over and over again. No, not *that* accusation. I've been accused of trying to be everybody's dad.

I don't know why some people think it's an insult. Personally, I take it as a compliment. What's more, I feel a sense of duty to those who need some form of paternal support. I don't feel like I had a dad growing up. The most positive male forces in my life were the men at church. My biological father and even my foster father were just other men in my life. I know that there are a lot of young men that feel the same way too, so if I can help them, I will.

During the pandemic, a young man who worked at my church was accused of a crime. I knew that he wasn't capable of that type of crime. This guy was a pushover, a small guy who wanted to stay out of everyone's way, but he had some substance abuse issues. The state that he was in at the time of his arrest inhibited him from properly communicating with the officers. I just knew, as I watched his trial, that we were victims of the same system.

His only crime was being poor. Poor and ignorant. He was ignorant to how the system operated and what he needed to do to work within it. I saw, based on the state of mind he was in and the suburb where he was arrested, that the police were going to be hard on him. On top of that, this young man didn't have the resources to contact a lawyer who would spend the necessary time on his case and give him the advice he needed to stay out of trouble. This man's only crime was being poor and ignorant and he was going to get punished for it.

The judge asked this young man to pay 10 percent upfront to cover a $20,000 bond. I knew this guy couldn't even come up with $200, so I asked the judge if I could say something in the Zoom meeting. She said yes.

"Your Honor, this is a steep bond. I just want to know what I have to do to keep this guy out of harm's way."

The judge was shocked to hear me speak up for this man. She assumed that the man wasn't going to make bail because this is how cases like his usually worked out. I know because I've seen quite a few of these court cases. The judges at this particular courthouse knew me, and they knew that if I showed up to support someone, the defendant likely had some credibility. But because we were on Zoom, my name didn't appear onscreen and no one saw my face. After asking my question and introducing myself, I let her know that the young man's bond was going to be paid in full.

This young man is not the only person I've been able to step in as a "dad." I've been a "dad" to many young men who have been falsely accused and faced sentencing just because they were poor or ignorant of how the criminal justice system worked. Sometimes, I pay their bond. Other times, I recruit the help of my sister who serves as general counsel. She doesn't practice the type of law that these young men are involved in, but she offers advice and treats them fairly. My sister talks to these young men the same way that the former U.S. Attorney talked to me, and these young men are more empowered because of her guidance.

This was not something that I did before I was placed in the dungeon. This is my recompense. I have become an advocate for people who have been falsely accused of crimes, and I have the language and ability to navigate this work because of my experiences. I have been blessed with this passion, and other people have been uplifted because of this blessing, too.

"You shall make the breastplate of judgment. Artistically woven according to the workmanship of the ephod you shall make it: of gold, blue, purple, and scarlet thread, and fine woven linen, you shall make it. It shall be doubled into a square: a span shall be its length, and a span shall be its width. And you shall put settings of stones in it, four rows of stones: The first row shall be a sardius, a topaz, and an emerald; this shall be the first row; the second row shall be a turquoise, a sapphire, and a diamond; the third row, a jacinth, an agate, and an amethyst; and the fourth row, a beryl, an onyx, and a jasper. They shall be set in gold settings. And the stones shall have the names of the sons of Israel, twelve according to their names, like the engravings of a signet, each one with its own name; they shall be according to the twelve tribes." (Exodus 28:15-21 NKJV)

Everything that I have done to give back to others has been a blessing, and inspired by God. And it has all led to the creation of the Cornerstone Christian Fellowship. A year after I was released from boot camp, I had a vision about the twelve precious stones. In that vision, the Lord told me that I was going to be a senior pastor. I was already an assistant pastor and a founding elder of my current church at the time. God told me that I had more steps to take. My journey was far from over.

He told me, "Tell your pastor that in twelve months you're going to start a church. Don't think about the resources you need or the location where this church will be built. Don't ask for any help. Go and start a church based on what I'm telling you about the twelve precious stones."

The Lord continued on, showing me the way forward. I was told to find twelve families who the church would nurture through the covenant. Anything that these families needed, we would provide. If they had recidivism issues, we would help them. If they had addiction issues, we would help them. Illiteracy, financial setbacks, financial knowledge–we would help them. Throughout my life, I have formed strategic relationships and built a network of people who have the resources to help in the way that I want to help people. In the same way that I have been advocating for young men who were falsely accused, I could help these families using that same network. In the end, we have all been blessed by it. As these families are supported and helped, the Lord told me, our church would only ask that they do the same for one person.

This vision that the Lord sent me has become the foundation of the ministry that I run today. We are a small, but growing ministry. When the Lord told me not to worry about resources, I listened. I pushed forward and I looked for a place where I could have church.

A friend who was involved in real estate heard about my search, and he sent me information about a building that was for sale. The building was worn down, but my friend told me maybe I could do something with it.

"Just go over there and look at it," he told me. Immediately, I started seeing good things. The building was located on Cypress Street. It was built into the landscape, made with cedar to evoke the image of the old rugged cross. The ceilings were high, cathedral ceilings. Yes, the building was in rough shape, the windows were broken, and it looked like an eyesore, but enough of the building was still intact. When you walked in, you felt the presence of The Lord. I knew that this was going to be our church, so I reached out to the owner.

I had raised around $80,000 to buy this building. At the time, the price was more than what it was worth. The owners initially were willing to take our calls. In the meantime, our ministry had to hold services in rented rooms and funeral homes that lent us their space while we waited for the sale of the building.

The owners stopped responding, but I was still determined to buy the building. I called and called. I must have called hundreds of times, with no answer. That didn't deter me. I wasn't giving up. This was our church! One Bible study, I reached out to a brother in the church named James Mattz. His family was one of the first twelve families that joined the ministry. James is a prominent real estate broker, so I knew he would be the best person to help me out as we secured this building.

"James, can you do me a favor? The owner of this building isn't calling me back. I want you to call the guy who has this building and tell him you may have a prospective buyer. Don't tell him you know me. Just tell them you have a client that wants to meet about it."

James agreed. By the following Sunday, he had secured a meeting with the owner. "Tomorrow," he told me, "you're going to go meet with him. And whatever you need this guy to sign, you take it with you." James had faith in the transaction. James and I were in agreement, and we knew that we were going to have a church by the end of that meeting.

The owner of the building's name was Mr. Burt, and I met with him the next day. He took one look at me and laughed. "Oh no, Pastor Keith!" he said. He knew exactly what James and I had cooked up. Now he had to face me!

"Mr. Burt," I told him, "first of all, I would like to apologize. I know I've called you 100 times about this building."

"No," he said, "you've called me 400 times!" We laughed. "But what I liked about you," he said, "is that you never left a curt message. I failed to call you back, but you never left me a message in anger. You were persistent. I respect that."

We had not made it to Mr. Burt's conference room, but I found myself compelled to ask him a question. "Mr. Burt, did you recently adopt some children?" I didn't know why that question came to me, but I let the Holy Spirit ask it.

"How did you know that?" he asked me. I'm sure he thought I had spent the whole morning Googling his life and family history. But I assured him that I hadn't.

"I don't really know," I told him. "I can't explain why I asked. I just have to attribute it to the Holy Spirit." I continued to tell him about my experience with adoption: calling out to God in the Robert Taylor Homes, being taken into my foster mother's home, and never being legally adopted but still calling Naomi "Mom."

As I told this story, Mr. Burt's face got redder and redder. He was flustered. All he could do was bring me into his conference room. We sat at a long, beautiful table in a long, beautiful room. Again, I felt compelled to speak.

"Mr. Burt, do you mind if we have a word of prayer?" He was still shaking, and he put his hands together. We prayed, and I assured him that the blessings of the Lord were not going to leave his house. Once our prayer was finished, I got down to brass tacks. I told Mr. Burt that keeping the building in the state that it was in was only going to be a liability for him. He agreed.

"How much can you give me today?" he asked.

I had raised $80,000 two months prior, but I let Mr. Burt know that the money was gone. "Here's what I'll do," I told him. Again, I felt compelled to say this. I don't know where it was coming from! "I'll give you $2,500 for the building. I can write a check for half today, and half at the end of the month. I've got to get this thing up to code, and it's only becoming a bigger problem." Mr. Burt sat back in his seat. For a moment, I almost doubted myself. But he stood up and shook my hand.

"Okay," he said. "You have a deal." And that's how we got our building.

"The wicked flee when no one pursues, but the righteous are bold as a lion. Because of the transgression of a land, many are its princes; but by a man of understanding and knowledge right will be prolonged." (Proverbs 28:1-2 NKJV)

I had worked in construction and I had many strategic relationships with people who worked in construction, so getting the building up to code shouldn't have been a problem. But the mayor of the town made it a problem. Churches don't pay taxes, so I was told that there was no way that another church was going to be built in the area. This was one of the final tests of my faith before we could officially open our doors. I knew the mayor wasn't right in what he said, so I continued to beg. I even showed up to where the mayor was having dinner one night and told him, "I have to have this church."

"Pastor Keith," he told me, "it's going to be easier for you to build a strip club than it will be for you to build a church. You better not get caught on that property holding services."

I was shook, but I didn't believe him. The man was violating my rights! I kept moving forward with the process. Even though he technically *couldn't* tell us that we couldn't use the building for a church, the mayor had the power to work with the city inspector and hit us with problem after problem. Every time the inspector came to look at the building, he gave me another long list of requests that I would have to address before we could hold services in the church. I worked in construction. I knew what it took to get a building up to code. This guy was just giving me a hard time because he had the mayor in his ear. He knew it and I knew it.

Week after week, I obliged the requests and put every last dime I had into fixing up the building. It still wasn't good enough. I was at my wit's end trying to resolve this issue, but the mayor wasn't budging. Changing his mind took every strategic relationship I had in the area. City council members listened to me, but assured me that the mayor was unmovable. Other pastors who knew the area knew I was dealing with an uphill battle. Finally, I was able to reach an architect for the city that could get in the mayor's ear. By this point, I was incensed. I had cried many tears over the struggle and I let this guy know I wasn't backing down.

"Look," I told the architect, "I've done the diplomatic thing. And I've done everything that I can in order to get my church open. But this guy is now violating my rights. I want you to tell him that I'm not just somebody that's going to roll over. I've exhausted my resources for the building. He's put me in a traumatic place; every time the city inspector agrees to get the building up to code, he comes back with contradicting requests. I've had lawyers come out to my house so I'm going to get some help. I'm going to get some relief. I worked for a prominent attorney who owned Heritage Bank Corporation. All of these people are going to help me, because the mayor is violating our rights as a church. I want to have church, even if it's just outside until everything gets resolved."

The architect shared that message with the mayor. The mayor heard him. He said we could have church outside the building until everything was fixed up. For twelve weeks after that phone call, we held church outside for two and a half hours every Sunday. Every Sunday we began with the prayer:

"Lord, we thank you for staying the rain, so that we can worship your name."

And every week, for twelve weeks, we stayed dry. On the twelfth week, no more than five minutes after we gave the benediction, the clouds started to form and the rain started to pour. But we were able to get through twelve weeks. On the thirteenth week, the church had been fixed up and we held our first Sunday service inside.

I thank the Lord for staying the rain so we could worship in His name.

We are still a growing ministry, still honoring our original mission centers on nurturing twelve families, with a significant focus on addressing hunger within our community. We achieve this by leveraging our extensive network to provide essential resources, guidance, and spiritual support. By prioritizing these twelve families, and ensuring they have access to nutritious food, we aim to create a ripple effect of love, care, and faith that extends throughout our congregation and beyond, embodying our commitment to living out the teachings of our faith in tangible, impactful ways.

Some families just need food to eat. That's okay, because we'll feed them. That's just what we do.

Not everyone understands how or why we do this. Other pastors will ask, "Why do you spend your time feeding people? You can't get grant money for cooking someone a meal." I always tell them the same thing. "I feed people because when I was a kid, I was hungry." We take care of the widows and children, clothe the naked, and feed the hungry. That's what we do, and we find a way to do it. I know very well that feeding people is not going to grow our ministry or bring in resources. But I can tell you how powerful it was to eat those first pancakes from scratch or have spaghetti dinners with my church. I want to have that same impact on all our families.

We are able to make this impact, even with limited resources, because we have coupled our actions with the Word and the power of God. We do what we can because that's what God wants us to do. The ministry is not a profit center. In fact, we're always asking for more so that we can give more. But when you're in God's rest, He'll send you His best. Whether his best is a deal on an eyesore of a building, a network that can bless the people in your life, or even reunification with your long-lost sister, God will send you His best. When you trust God unequivocally, you know that He can provide beyond anything you can ever ask for. We know that because we see it every day.

There is no need to worry. I don't worry. Worry negates prayer. If you're worrying, don't pray. And if you're praying, don't worry. My trust in faith is to focus on the needs, and Him exceeding that which we need. Time and time again, He has proven that He will do this. I have received so much recompense from Him, but I know that with the ministry, He is just getting started in terms of what He will provide for us, our families, and our community. I trust in Him, just as I have trusted in Him from climbing those thirteen flights of stairs.

Final Thoughts

"For the thing I greatly feared has come upon me, and what I dreaded has happened to me. I am not at ease, nor am I quiet; I have no rest, for trouble comes." (Job 3:25-26 NKJV)

W hen people discuss the story of Job, they say that God was testing Job. But the story of Job is actually a story about fear. In the last lines of the story, Job talks about what he greatly feared. There were times in my life when I felt fear. I felt fear, as a child, living in Robert Taylor Homes. I felt fear when I was accused of criminal activity. I felt fear, but I never gave into that fear. Fear is the opposite of faith. Fear counteracts faith. We can spend as much time as we want, listening to the rumblings of gossip or threats to what we love. But with faith, we do not have to fear.

Every time I felt fear, starting at the moment that I cried out to God on those thirteen flights of stairs, I was saved. God showed me that there is no need for fear when you have faith.

What does it take to activate our faith? Love. God is love. Let me tell you this again, because I need you to really take this in: God is love. God loves everybody; He alienates nobody. Every single person that I've told you about, from my biological parents to my foster parents to my teachers to people that tried to take me down a dark path, they are all loved by God. Every person that supported me while I was in the dungeon *and* the people that put me there in the first place are loved by God. Love activates our faith, and if we want to overcome fear and let our faith lead the way, we have to love.

Loving somebody that you already like is easy. It's no big deal. I had no problem loving my parents and my teachers and the men at my church who guided me toward Christ. But in the times where I was tested by God, I was given the task of truly loving all people. I'm not telling you that you have to put yourself in harm's way or operate outside of wisdom. I always kept my wits about me when I worked with men in the mortgage business, as an activist, and even in boot camp. But when you love people, even the ones that spitefully use you, you are breaking the chains that bind you. Hatred binds you. It makes you a different type of slave. Love sets you free.

God is love, and God loves all people. If I have the Word of God in me, and I hate people, I'm lying to myself about something. Holding hate in my heart and claiming that I live by the Word of God makes no sense. I can't hate someone based on their race or sexual orientation or political party. My beliefs may lead me to vote for one politician or the other, but it's because my beliefs are based on what the Word of God says. I don't have an original opinion outside the Word of God, I just don't. And I'm not the person to put anyone in heaven or hell, ridicule them, or love them any less. I want all people to experience heaven, because I love them, because God is love.

I have reached this conclusion after living many years of growing, learning, and studying the Word of God. Throughout my life, I have made mistakes. Everyone has made mistakes. That's what humans do. But now, I place my whole self in faith. I act not out of fear, but out of faith. Not out of hate, but out of love. I strive for this. I don't always achieve it, even to this day. But I believe that I have been called according to my purpose, and my purpose is not to complain and to take full responsibility for the mistakes I have made. The technical violation which resulted in charges against me was the result of a mistake. In business, sometimes we take risks. And the rules are different for some who take risks than they are for others. I know, based on the professional opinions of those around me, that men who made the same choices I made were not charged for those choices. But I know I should have handled things differently, even if I never acted with criminal intent. There was a level of detail that I should have paid attention to. I should have made different choices relating to the business partner I had in this particular transaction.

All of that is behind me now, because I have faith. I activate my faith with love, and I know that only I have the responsibility to make those choices and to live my life as a man of God.

After everything that I have been through, I don't always make perfect choices, but I act out of love because I have faith.

Romans 8:28 (NKJV) says, *"And we know that all things work together for good to those who love God, to those who are the called according to His purpose."*

If you had read me this Bible verse the day after I had been accused of fraud and my world turned upside down, I might not have emphatically agreed with you. Grappling with this verse took time. I never would have said that going to boot camp and leaving the mortgage business would be things that worked together for good.

The early days of boot camp were tough. I was in decent shape, but I was much older than the other guys in the facility and there were times I thought I wasn't going to make it. And then one day, in the barracks, I looked down and asked what this was all about. Why was I here? What was God's plan for me?

The Holy Spirit responded. I felt like the Holy Spirit was speaking to me. "Submit to the process" is what I heard. And I did. In prison, out of prison, in real estate, in starting a ministry, and in jumping through hoops just to get a church up and running. I submit to the process. And as I submit to the process, things begin to work themselves out.

After that moment, I finally felt like I was at rest. Before, I had been in turmoil. I was stressed, worried about what my time in the dungeon meant for my life and my purpose. I couldn't enter God's rest because I was worried! I had to find a way to understand that my burdens were not mine to bear–I had to submit to the process. Everything was on God, and God was at His best.

Every time the odds are stacked against you, that is when God is at his best. He never puts you through more than you can handle. When you become overwhelmed, you need to know that he is able to abundantly provide more than you can ask. We can have faith that He will take on all of our burdens. He can, and He will, but only if we have faith in Him. Don't put your faith in chariots. Don't put your faith in the military. Don't put your faith in strength. Your faith belongs in the creator of them all.

I put my faith in God when I was on those thirteen flights of stairs so many, many years ago. Time and time again, I have put my faith in Him and He has delivered. I urge you to put your faith in Him, too. If you take away anything from this book, from my silly stories and the honest recollection of my struggles, take this lesson away. Put your faith in Him, and He will return the favor.

If you would like to send me your thoughts on the book or book me to speak, email me here: keith@fromfostertofavor.com.